Bear Grylls

EXTREME PLANET

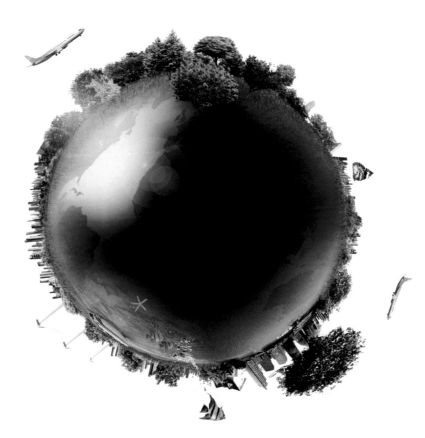

Bear Grylls

EXTREME PLANET

Exploring the Most Extreme Stuff on Earth

Bear Grylls
EXTREME PLANET
Exploring the Most Extreme Stuff on Earth

I've been so lucky in my life to have traveled to many of the great extremes of our planet, experiencing the subzero temperatures of the Polar regions, the blistering heat of the deserts, and a whole lot in between. But there's more to marvel at than just temperatures – did you know that the darkest cave on Earth is filled with unique species of blind bugs? Or that there are thunderstorms in Honduras that literally rain fishes? There are raging rivers and parched plains, animals immense and microscopic, fish that fly, birds that deep-sea dive, and so much more.

As I've explored and adventured, above all I've been impressed with the resilience of nature. Our planet can teach us so many lessons about surviving and adapting, but I believe our great calling is to make sure that we now work together to protect it.

This book will teach you everything there is to know about how nature survives and adapts to the planet's most extreme conditions, and how animals change to fit into their environments. I've also packed it full of survival tips and tricks that I have learned from my travels – extreme advice to survive almost any extreme situation.

Our planet is an incredible place and life is best lived as a great adventure, so let's get out there and explore!

CONTENTS

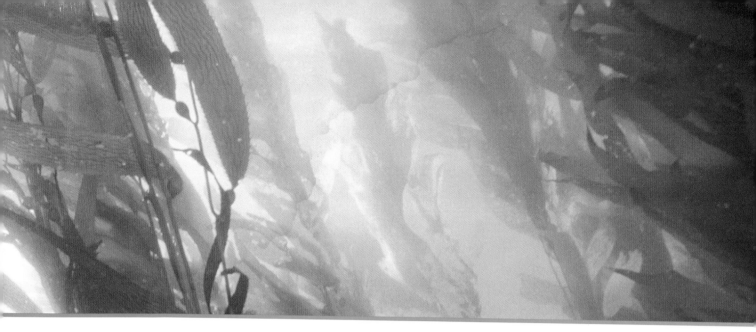

ANIMALIA

Some of the biggest and best bits from the animal kingdom

Walk this way

Millipedes are the leggiest critters. They have up to 400 tiny legs, but can't walk very fast. Centipedes, their close relatives, have between 20 and 300 legs.

All mixed up

When scientists first saw an Australian platypus, they thought someone had stitched it together as a prank. It has a rubbery beak like a duck, feet like an otter, and a tail like a beaver. Along with the echidnas, it is the only mammal in the world that lays eggs. It is also one of the world's few venomous mammals – the males have a poison-filled spike on their back feet.

BEAR SAYS

The scariest animals are crocodiles, with their vicious teeth and powerful muscles.

Longest tongue

Can you clean your ears with your tongue? Giraffes can! They have the longest neck of any animal, about 6 feet, and the longest tail (up to 8 feet). Why were they once called "camel-leopards"? Because their head looks like a camel head, they can go a long time without drinking water, and they have spots like a leopard!

THE FACE ONLY A MOTHER COULD LOVE!

EARS: Elephants have the world's biggest ears. They flap them like fans, to keep themselves cool.

HORNS: The water buffalo from Southeast Asia has the longest horns – up to 79 inches from tip to tip.

EYES: Colossal squid have the world's biggest eyes – bigger than dinner plates, at about 11 inches wide. These deep-sea dwellers need them to see in dark water, as they can live at over 6,500 feet deep.

TEETH: Sharks have the deadliest teeth. Not just one row, but several rows that keep growing and moving forward to replace old ones that wear out. They lose about 30,000 teeth in their lifetime.

MOUSTACHE: The prize for the neatest, nicest moustache goes to the emperor tamarin monkey, from the Amazon.

BEAR SAYS

What do an ant colony and a pride of lions have in common? Teamwork.

Lethal legs

The longest, strongest bird's legs belong to African ostriches. They can run at 45 mph! And they cover 10–16 feet in a single stride. These birds can kick you to death with their long, sharp toe claws.

INTO THE DEEP

It's time for an underwater adventure!

Deepest trench

The world's biggest ocean trench, the Mariana Trench, is so deep that if you stacked Mt. Everest PLUS the world's tallest building, the Burj Khalifa of the United Arab Emirates, PLUS the Great Pyramid of Giza in Egypt on top of that, PLUS the world's tallest statue, the Spring Temple Buddha in China, on top of that, there would still be almost 3,300 feet of water above it!

BEAR SAYS

Two of my most extreme challenges have been climbing Everest and swimming in semi-frozen lakes!

Mount Everest is Earth's highest mountain, located in the Himalayan Mountains in Nepal and Tibet.

29,029 ft.

35,797 ft.

The Mariana Trench is the deepest point in the ocean.

Deepest ocean voyage
In 1960, an underwater vehicle known as a bathyscaphe ("deep ship") made it down as deep as people can ever go. The ship was called the *Trieste*, and in it were Swiss oceanographer Jacques Piccard and US Navy Lieutenant Don Walsh. They reached the floor of the Mariana Trench in the Pacific Ocean, 35,797 feet below the surface.

Don't breathe out
Can you hold your breath for more than 100 minutes? Don't actually try it! That's what elephant seals do when they dive down for food. The deep-diving record by a seal goes to a southern elephant seal, spotted 7,835 feet beneath the waves.

Ain't no sunshine
In 1977, scientists in a submarine found holes in the bottom of the ocean, spewing out boiling water from within the Earth. They also found bacteria living there – just about the only life on Earth that doesn't depend on the Sun. The bacteria live on the chemical energy in the boiling water.

DEEP DIVERS

Deepest human free dive
328 ft.

Deepest diving bird
1,854 ft.

Deepest diving reptile
2,100 ft.

Deepest diving mammal
8,200 ft.

BEAR SAYS
Scuba stands for self-contained underwater breathing apparatus. The amazing record for the deepest scuba dive 1,090 feet.

SOUTH AMERICA

The Amazon rain forest covers more than 2.5 million square miles. That's over a billion acres. It is nearly as big as Australia. It covers about half of Brazil, as well as some of Venezuela, Colombia, eastern Ecuador, and Peru. No other place on Earth is richer in life. More than one-third of all species in the world live here, including over 500 mammal, 175 lizard, and over 300 other reptile species... oh, and millions of insect varieties.

"He who kills in one leap"
Jaguars are the biggest cats in South America. They kill by leaping on prey from a sneaky spot. They are fine tree climbers and not bad swimmers.

Gimme some air
The Amazon rain forest is nicknamed the "lungs of the planet." Its billions of trees produce 20% of the world's oxygen, which we need to breathe.

I'd like to sssquash you...
Be careful of anacondas here, the world's biggest snake. These 25-foot-long giants can wrap themselves around you, crush you, and then gobble you whole, head first. But it's just a baby compared to the monster snake fossil that scientists found in a coal mine in Colombia in 2008. It was as long as a bus and weighed as much as a small car. Lucky it lived 60 million years ago!

6,000,000,000,000,000

That's how many sheets of paper you could make from the wood in all the trees in the Amazon.

BEAR SAYS

Bird-eating spiders are not as strange a snack as they sound! They are packed with protein.

JUNGLE FEVER

The Amazon rain forest is the world's biggest and most AMAZING jungle

Head shrinkers
The Shuar people in Ecuador and Peru used to shrink the heads of people they killed. They would take out the skull, sew up the eyes and mouth, then boil the flesh before drying it. The Shuar thought they could get hold of the person's soul by shrinking their head.

Canopy capers
This incredibly vast jungle is so thick that very little sunlight reaches the forest floor, and very few plants actually live down there. Most of the action takes place at the top of the trees, called the canopy. Some animals live all their lives up there and never come down to the ground.

Feeling peckish?
Kids from the Piaroa tribe in Venezuela hunt 11-inch goliath bird-eating spiders out of their burrows, roast them, then munch on their legs!

No TV or phones here
The Amazon rain forest is so huge that there are still thousands of people living in it who have never had contact with the modern outside world.

Titan tummy
Titan beetles are enormous. Their bodies can grow 6.5 inches long. With such a huge tummy, you would think they have a monster appetite to match. Curiously, the adult male titan never eats. It simply flies around looking to match up with a female titan until it dies!

LIVING IN EXTREMES

Over 7 billion people live on planet Earth, in the most surprising places...

Most NORTHERLY capital
Reykjavík, Iceland: 1,786 miles from the North Pole.

Most SOUTHERLY capital
Wellington, New Zealand: 3,368 miles from the South Pole.

160°F
HOTTEST LAND SURFACE TEMPERATURE EVER RECORDED
Dasht-e Lut, Iran. You could fry an egg on this!

136°F
HOTTEST AIR TEMPERATURE EVER RECORDED
Al-Aziziya, Libya. Way too hot to go to school!

122°F
HOTTEST PLACE WHERE PEOPLE LIVE
The Tuareg people have adapted to living in this heat in Africa's Sahara desert. They live in tents, wear loose robes, and ride on camels.

High there
La Rinconada, in Peru, is the world's highest city, at 16,728 feet above sea level. It's higher up than Europe's highest mountain, Mont Blanc, at 15,781 feet high!

-53°F
COLDEST CITY IN THE WORLD
If you live in Yakutsk, Siberia, you might need to wear a few pairs of underpants and lots of layers of fur and wool when you go out to play... because this is how unbelievably cold it often gets in this Russian city. It's a good place to snuggle up with a Siberian husky.

A bit chilly!
The coldest temperature ever measured was at Vostok Station, a Russian research station in Antarctica. The temperature was -128.6°F on July 21, 1983.

BEAR ...YS

In any extreme environment, keep calm, face your fear, and plan ahead.

Going to HIGH school

The Pumaqangtang Primary School in Tibet is the highest school in the world! At 3.4 miles above sea level, it's not great if you get altitude sickness. There are lots of snow blizzards, and it can get as cold as -40°F.

BOTTOM school

The most southerly school in the world is on the tip of Antarctica, at a remote research station called Esperanza Base. The school is run by Argentina, so the lessons are in Spanish.

Checking in

At 13,000 feet, the Everest View Hotel in Nepal is the highest hotel in the world.

Poles apart

It's about 12,430 miles from the North Pole to the South Pole.

High and low

Ecuador, in South America, is the only country in the world where the temperature reaches zero at zero degrees latitude. Although it sits right on the equator, there are icy glaciers on its mountain peaks.

PINKEST AND PURPLEST

Pretty astonishing things come in shades of pink and purple

Rosiest waters

The world's pinkest lake is Lac Rose (Rose Lake), also called Lake Retba, in the African nation of Senegal. Its unusual pinkness is caused by bacteria that thrive in its highly salty waters. People harvest salt from the lake.

Bloom bloom bloom

Every year, people in Japan eagerly await cherry blossom season, which starts in March to May. They love to picnic under the trees, in centuries-old flower-viewing ("*hanami*") festivals.

Happy snappy poop

Huge, heavy, pinky-purply hippos love wallowing in African water holes to stay cool. Here's another cool thing about them: hippo sweat is pink! Hippos might look cute and cuddly, but these hefty vegetarians kill more people in Africa than any other large animal. If a hippo yawns and shows you its huge pink throat and long sharp teeth, run for your life – it is telling you it is super cranky! Those strong jaws can bite a crocodile in half. And if that doesn't scare you off, a hippo might pull a really dirty trick by spraying poop all over you.

Spikiest mouthful
Purple sea urchins are some of the prickliest creatures in the sea. They live for up to 30 years. Otters love to eat them. So do people in Japan and Sicily.

Volcano lizard
Pink land iguanas are very rare. They live only on the Volcan Wolf volcano in the Galápagos Islands.

Plump lump
The Indian purple frog was only discovered in 2003. Scientists say it is a living fossil, because it looks like its ancient ancestors. It is nicknamed the pig-nose frog or doughnut frog.

Furry scaly fairy story
The rare pichiciego from Argentina is one of the most peculiar creatures ever. It looks like a furry hamster, but it has a shell of pink bony scales along its back, and pink scaly feet with the hugest claws. Also called a pink fairy armadillo, it is the smallest member of the armadillo family, and will fit in your hand. When it is scared, it can burrow into sand in seconds, thanks to its massive claws.

Berry crazy
The biggest purple berry is actually eaten all around the world as a vegetable. The eggplant, or aubergine, is native to India, where it is known as brinjal. Back in the old days, people thought eating it made you insane.

Go batty

Every summer evening, more than 20 million bats zoom out of Bracken Cave in Texas to feed. It takes three hours for all the tiny critters in the world's largest bat colony to get out of the cave. The swarm even shows up on the radar of the local airport. The hungry little Mexican free-tailed bats gobble 276 tons of insects a night.

INCREDIBLE CAVES

So much more than just a big hole in the ground... some people even dive into them!

Pirate treasure

Back in the 1600s, pirates in the Bahamas really did hide treasures they stole from passing ships. Where? In caves, of course, in the thousands of islands that make up the Bahamas. Who knows, some of it could still be hidden away!

Black and smelly

A cave in Romania, discovered in 1986, is crawling with blind spiders, scorpions, leeches and millipedes, all sealed off and living in complete darkness. It's the only known ecosystem on land that doesn't need sunlight. The animals live on bacteria that get their energy from sulfur!

Crystal playgrounds

Climbing up and down and around the truly giant white crystals in Mexico's Cave of Crystals makes you feel really tiny. Some crystals are up to 36 feet long – six times longer than a tall man.

BEAR SAYS

Gomantong Caves, in Malaysia, boast a 100-foot pile of bat poop. What a stink!

Ancient art

Chauvet Cave in France has the oldest cave art in the world. Some of the paintings on the walls are 32,000 years old. It even has paintings of species that are now extinct, such as a megaceros (a huge elk) and mammoths.

Do drop in

The Vrtoglavica Cave in Slovenia has the world's deepest single vertical drop: 1,978 feet. The Empire State Building in New York or the Petronas Towers in Malaysia would easily fit in it. However, the Cave of Swallows in Mexico is the world's largest cave shaft, because it is very wide, as well as 1,094 feet deep – deep enough to swallow New York's 1,047-foot Chrysler Building. People BASE jump into it.

MAKING A SPLASH

A whole world of watery adventure!

Blue holes all around

People love exploring the famous "blue holes" in our seas and oceans. These deep round holes, where the ocean floor suddenly drops away, are called "sinkholes."

At the bottom of the beautiful 410-foot Great Blue Hole off Belize (main picture) are natural underwater passageways, where you can see stalactites and even old fossils – but to get there you have to swim through a layer of poisonous gas.

The 426-foot-deep Red Sea Blue Hole, off the coast of Egypt, is famous for its beautiful fish and coral. It is also nicknamed the "world's deadliest dive" and "diver's cemetery." At least 40 divers have died there.

The deepest seawater sinkhole is the 663-foot Dean's Blue Hole, in the Bahamas, where people often try to break the world free-diving record – 331 feet on a single breath of air.

Diving the icy rift

You'll need to put on a very warm "dry suit" to go diving in Iceland's famous Silfra Rift. The Silfra fissure in Iceland's Thingvellir National Park is a great crack between the two big tectonic plates that sit underneath Europe and North America. You can dive in this deep crack, as parts of it are full of water that is extremely pure and clear – and only just above freezing. The crack is getting wider, as these two tectonic plates are drifting about 0.75 inch farther apart every year.

Sharkiest dive
South Africa's Shark Alley is nicknamed the "great white shark capital of the world." Here, thrill-seekers jump into steel cages off the side of boats to go swimming with lots of awesomely big great white sharks.

✗ BEAR SAYS
Take care around water! I once came close to death in a fast-flowing river in the Sumatran jungle.

Swimming with crocs
Lake Argyle is Australia's largest human-made lake. And it's full of crocodiles: about 25,000 of them! The crocs don't usually eat people, but they can give you a nasty nip. So when you are competing in the world's biggest freshwater swimming marathon – the 12-mile Lake Argyle Classic – you might want to swim just that little bit faster!

The ghost beetle from Southeast Asia is the whitest natural object on Earth. Scientists are studying it to learn how to make other things whiter.

The blackest thing in the world is a sheet of tiny carbon tubes, made in a US laboratory. It is 30 times blacker than what scientists call "black."

Stripe me lucky

The striped patterns on zebras are unique to each zebra – just like fingerprints. These wild African horses have never really been tamed. They sleep standing up.

Stop press!

What's black and white and read all over? A newspaper, of course. The biggest-selling newspaper in the world is *Yomiuri Shimbun*, from Japan, which sells more than 13 million copies every single day.

Bamboozle snoozer

China's immensely shy giant pandas are one of the world's rarest mammals. They love to eat. They spend about 6 hours a day chowing down on bamboo and, er, more bamboo. And when they are not eating, they are usually asleep.

BLACK AND WHITE

Sometimes the world really is black and white

Tiger, tiger, burning white
White tigers are rarely seen in the wild. Usually they are only seen in zoos. Their very unusual coloring comes from a genetic defect from inbreeding.

Smelly bellies
North American skunks are famous for their repulsive pong. Whenever they feel threatened, they aim their bottom at the nearest offender, raise their tail, and squirt a diabolically stinky oily spray at them, from up to 10 feet away. The smell can linger for days.

TRAPPED IN TIME

We are all time travelers

Looking up at the sky at night is like looking into a time machine. The light we can see from the stars has often been traveling for millions of years before it reaches Earth. Perhaps some of the stars do not even exist anymore.

160 million years ago

That's sick!

Scientists in England discovered vomit from an ichthyosaur in Peterborough. Ichthyosaurs were marine reptiles that lived at the same time as dinosaurs, about 160 million years ago. The spew was made up of the remains of shellfish.

Fowl tasting

If you want to find out what that terrifying dinosaur, Tyrannosaurus rex, would taste like, eat a chicken. That's because chickens are modern-day descendants of the T. rex!

BEAR SAYS

Navigating by the stars is a key survival skill. Mastering it could save your life.

80 million years ago
Feathered find
A thin strand of "hair" trapped in an 80-million-year-old piece of amber found near Alberta, Canada, turned out to be the world's earliest known feather from an ancient bird. You might also find insects trapped in amber, as well as flowers and leaves.

BEAR SAYS
I don't fancy my chances in a real-life Jurassic Park. Dinosaurs were bigger, faster, and more powerful!

10,000 years ago
Mammoth task
The bodies of woolly mammoths that lived more than 10,000 years ago have been found preserved in the frozen soil of Siberia. Scientists hope that one day they can extract DNA from them and bring them back to life, in a real-life Jurassic Park.

4,500 years ago
All wrapped up
Rich and powerful people in ancient Egypt were mummified after they died, so they could travel to the afterlife. Their organs were removed through a slit in the side of their body, and their brain was dragged out through their nose, using a long hook. Then their bodies were dried out and wrapped in special sheets. Really important people such as pharaohs and queens were buried in pyramids, such as the Great Pyramid of Giza, in Egypt.

2,500 years ago
Looking good for their age
The bodies of people found in bogs of northern Europe can be up to 2,500 years old, and are often perfectly preserved. It appears that many of them were murdered before their bodies were thrown into the swamps.

700,500,000,000,000,000,000

That's how many grains of sand there are on the world's beaches, according to mathematicians at the University of Hawaii. And that doesn't include the sand in any deserts!

LIFE'S A BEACH!

Relax and have a splash...

That's plane crazy

You'd better be careful where you lie down if you go sunbathing at Maho Beach, on the island of St. Maarten in the Caribbean. The island's airport is right next to the beach – and huge planes skim just a few feet above the sand while landing... often blowing beachgoers right off their feet!

Rainbow beaches

The beaches of Harbour Island in the Bahamas have beautiful pink sand, thanks to the coral mixed through it. Vik Beach in Iceland is covered in volcanic black sand and flat black stones and pebbles; there are also eerie dark rocky outcrops sticking out of the water, like wicked witches' hats. Olivine crystals from a volcanic explosion are responsible for the green sand on Hawaii's Papakolea Beach. Then there's Red Beach on the Greek island of Santorini, which – you guessed it – has red sand. Minerals leaching onto Pfeiffer Beach in California have turned some of its sand bright purple.

BEAR SAYS

Explore! At low tide, with an adult, look in tide pools for fish, barnacles, and crabs. Don't disturb them though, just observe. Their world is incredible!

Dinosaurs in the cliffs

Take a walk along the Jurassic Coast, in southwest England, and you are sure to come face-to-face with a dinosaur. The sea has washed away the land, leaving layer after layer of ancient fossils exposed. The first pterodactyl – a giant flying reptile – was found here.

Lots of pop

The world's bubbliest beach could very well be Champagne Beach in Dominica. Tiny bubbles rise constantly from the volcanic sea floor, creating an effect like a glass of fizzy soda pop. It's a great place to go snorkeling.

Ocean under cover

If you are worried about sunburn, try having a swim at the world's largest indoor beach. Ocean Dome, in Miyazaki, southern Japan, is 984 feet long and 328 feet wide. Its roof has a beautiful blue sky painted on it, there's a flame-spitting volcano next to it, and the most perfect blue water laps onto fake sand that doesn't stick to you like the real stuff does.

Dig for a swim

Hot Water Beach, on New Zealand's Coromandel Peninsula, is a great place for a dip in the middle of winter. Rather than swimming in the sea, beachgoers dig holes in the sand, which fill with warm mineral waters. They can then have a nice warm soak, no matter how cold the air temperature is.

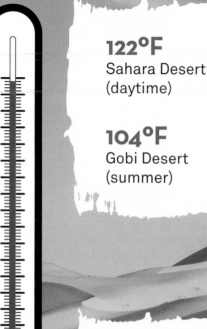

122°F
Sahara Desert
(daytime)

104°F
Gobi Desert
(summer)

-40°F
Gobi Desert
(winter)

Freezing desert

Although it's freezing cold and permanently packed with ice, Antarctica is also the largest desert in the world! The Antarctic desert covers an area of 5.3 million square miles, which is much larger than Europe, the US, or Australia. It is called a desert because it receives less than 10 inches of rain each year.

BEAR SAYS

To keep cool in the desert, soak a rag in water (or pee) then wrap it around your head.

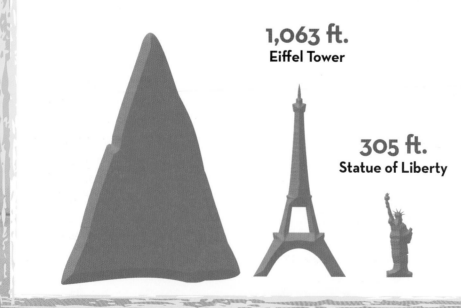

1,526 ft.
Isaouane-n-Tifernine

1,063 ft.
Eiffel Tower

305 ft.
Statue of Liberty

Grand sands

When the wind blows across the vast sandy deserts of North Africa, it creates huge seas of sand that look like a golden ocean. These big "waves" of sand are called dunes. Some of the world's tallest sand dunes are in a part of the Sahara Desert called Isaouane-n-Tifernine in Algeria, and are up to 1,526 feet tall. Imagine trying to climb them!

Got the chop
The world's loneliest tree was more than 250 miles from any other tree, but that didn't stop a drunk driver from knocking it down with his truck in 1973. A steel monument now stands in the Sahara Desert in Niger where the Tree of Ténéré once grew.

Not all deserts are barren
The Sonoran Desert in North America has more than 2,000 plant species, and over 550 different species of mammals, birds, amphibians, reptiles, fish, and insects.

Dangerous drink
Thousands of thirsty camels risk a horrible death when they take a drink at Guelta d'Archei in Chad. Lurking in its waters are lots of hungry crocodiles! A guelta is a water hole that forms in the desert from underground springs.

DESERTS

Our driest spots are dazzlingly different

High and dry
It's hard to believe that this boat once hauled in fish from the Aral Sea, which lies between Kazakhstan and Uzbekistan. But the sea has shrunk, leaving boats marooned on dry land – some more than 60 miles from the water's edge.

Hot to trot
The world's toughest footrace takes place in Death Valley, California, one of the hottest deserts in the world, where temperatures hit 122°F in the shade. About 80 people start the 135-mile Badwater Ultramarathon, but one-third don't finish.

Stick with it

Stick insects are brilliant at melting into their surroundings. Their bodies and legs look like sticks and twigs. Because the insects resemble plants, predators just ignore them.

NOT WHAT IT SEEMS

Super-sharp survival tactics

Razzle dazzle

Some animals use a type of camouflage called dazzle. Zebras' stripes are an example of this. When zebras in herds run from a predator, their stripes make it hard for the predator to judge the zebras' speed and direction, making it more likely they can escape. However, this type of camouflage makes them easier to spot when standing still.

That's all white

Polar bears can't change their color, but that doesn't matter because they live in places that are usually snow-white! Being white makes it easy for them to sneak up on prey. They also have an amazingly sharp sense of smell to sniff out animals hiding below the ice.

BEAR SAYS

My top survival tip is always to stay calm and think smart. Panic leads to poor decisions, and that's the most dangerous thing of all!

See-through skin

A chameleon's skin is see-through. It is the cells underneath its skin that let a chameleon change its color. While chameleons sometimes change their color to blend in with their surroundings, the color changes are used mainly for communication. A calm chameleon might be green, while an angry chameleon might be yellow or orange. They can also do weird things with their eyes. Each eye can move by itself, so chameleons can look in two directions at once. They really do have eyes in the back of their head!

Many animals in one

The mimic octopus, which lives in the sea off the Indonesian coast, is one of the world's greatest tricksters. The octopus can change its shape, color, and movements to copy more than 15 different dangerous marine animals. It can make itself look like a giant crab, a lionfish, a stingray, and even a banded sea snake! It changes its look to try to scare off predators.

Sole survivor

What are the chances? Flat fish, such as sole, grow both eyes on one side of their body! They lie on the seafloor and keep a lookout with both eyes for things that might gobble them up. It looks like they are lying on their belly, but they are really lying on one side.

Split personality

During mating season, cuttlefish develop a split personality. During the day, the skins of male cuttlefish flash in bright contrasting patterns and colors to impress the females and warn off rivals. But at night they use their colorful skin skills to hide from predators, by mimicking the color, shape, and texture of their surroundings. So if they hide near a rock at night, they will be the same color and texture as rock. Or they'll look just like sand if they are resting on the ocean floor.

BUG'S LIFE

The strangest facts about the most curious critters

Weta whopper!

The largest insect in the world is so big it eats carrots! But it is also very rare. The giant weta is found only on Little Barrier Island in New Zealand. It looks a bit like a huge grasshopper. It can weigh up to 2.5 ounces, about the same as three mice! Its body can be 4 inches long.

Taken for a ride

Before a jewel wasp lays its eggs, it has to take a cockroach for a ride! The wasp stings a cockroach to make it sleepy, then rides it into the cockroach's burrow, steering it in with its own long antennae. The wasp then lays its eggs in the cockroach's stomach and shuts it in the burrow with rocks until the eggs hatch.

Too many to count

Scientists reckon that most of the insect species on the planet still haven't been discovered. They believe there are more than 9 million different types of insects – that's 75% of all animal species. A new type of insect is discovered, on average, every hour!

Can't see me, can't see you

The smallest insects are male fairyflies. These tiny wasps from Costa Rica grow to only 0.005 inch – much smaller than a grain of salt. They have no wings, can't see, and they live on the eggs of other insects. Female wasps are twice as big as males.

Male fairyfly magnified 100 times

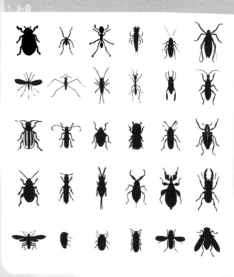

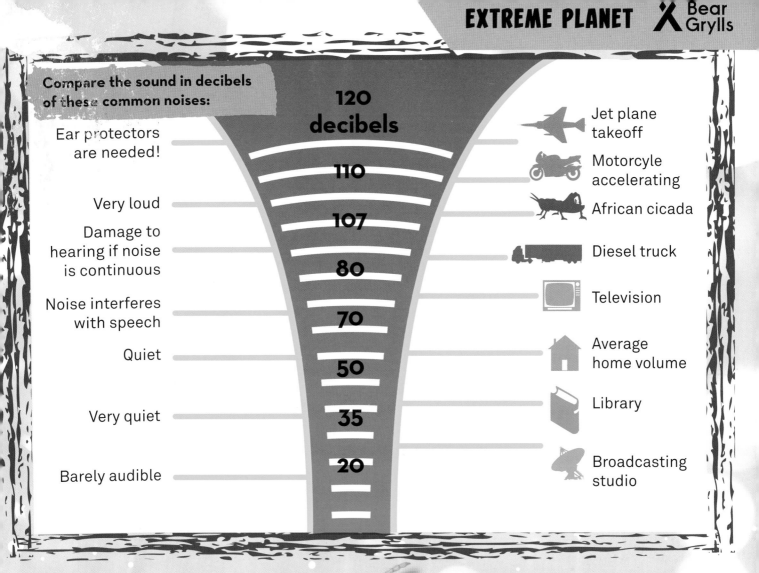

Compare the sound in decibels of these common noises:

120 decibels

110

107

80

70

50

35

20

Ear protectors are needed!

Very loud

Damage to hearing if noise is continuous

Noise interferes with speech

Quiet

Very quiet

Barely audible

Jet plane takeoff

Motorcyle accelerating

African cicada

Diesel truck

Television

Average home volume

Library

Broadcasting studio

Weird and wonderful

The giraffe weevil is not only a weird-looking thing, it also probably has the longest head of any insect. This strange insect is from the island of Madagascar. The male weevil nods his big head around to try to interest a mate, while the females roll a leaf around their head before laying eggs in the leaf.

Feats of strength

The hercules beetle is so strong it can lift 850 times its own body weight. That would be like us lifting an army tank or a giant dinosaur.

HOT STUFF

Cool facts about the hottest things

BEAR SAYS

In hot weather, your key battle is to stay hydrated. Always drink plenty of fresh water.

Hotter than the Sun

The highest temperature ever recorded on Earth was produced in Sandia National Laboratories in California. The temperature of 3.6 billion °F was created in 2006 in a massive X-ray machine. This is far hotter even than the Sun, which burns at a mere 27 million °F.

Hot footing it

On the Fijian island of Beqa, locals walk barefoot over stones heated in a fire until they are white-hot. Legend says that the islanders were given this power over fire by a spirit god. In other parts of Fiji, Indian Fijians also walk on hot coals, during a Hindu religious festival.

Get cracking

You can cook eggs in Dominica's Boiling Lake. The lake, in Morne Trois Pitons National Park, is on a volcano. The superhot steam that is forced through the blue-gray water makes it bubble and spit in the middle, where it is deepest.

Hot, hot, hot!

Death Valley, in California, is probably the consistently hottest place on Earth, with an average summer temperature of 117°F. The hottest air temperature ever recorded was 136°F in Al-Aziziyah, Libya, in 1922. Dasht-e Lut in Libya is a very dry and very hot desert plateau. In some parts, nothing lives – not even bacteria!

Warm welcome

The Afar people live in one of the hottest and most inhospitable places on Earth – the Danakil Depression in Africa. It is part of the Great Rift, 394 feet below sea level, where temperatures reach 145°F. The earth is cracked, lava oozes up from below, and tremors regularly shake the ground. The Afar are nomads, herding goats, camels, and cattle.

Hot in the city

Although it doesn't get the extreme temperatures of some cities, Thailand's capital, Bangkok, is the hottest city when judged by year-round heat. Temperatures are often above 104°F day and night. The city's air is very polluted, which traps the heat!

Playing with fire

Some people like to fill their mouths with fuel and blow it out in a big stream of flame. Others like to take burning rods and put them out by swallowing the fire. They are called fire-breathers and fire-eaters, and both of them can end up with a blistery mouth and a burned tongue. Ouch!

Tongue blaster

The hottest chili in the world is the Trinidad moruga scorpion. These golf-ball-size chilies are about 240 times hotter than a jalapeño. You should wear gloves and perhaps even a mask when cooking with these fireballs.

16 seconds of terror

If you're not keen on heights, then you won't want to peer over the edge of Mt. Thor, in Canada. It is famous for having the world's longest purely vertical drop. Leap off the top and you won't touch Earth again until you've fallen 4,101 feet. (It will take about 16 seconds.)

TAKE A PEAK

Huge facts about the world's mighty mountains

These presidents really rock

Four giant heads are carved into the rocky cliffs of Mt. Rushmore in South Dakota. The huge sculptures show previous American presidents George Washington, Thomas Jefferson, Theodore Roosevelt, and Abraham Lincoln. Workers back in the 1920s and 1930s used dynamite and jackhammers to carve most of the features, and had to hang off ropes to do the work. Each head is about 60 feet tall.

Hiding its height

We all know Mt. Everest in the Himalayas is the world's tallest mountain, right? Maybe not! Measured from base to peak, Hawaii's Mauna Kea pips Mt. Everest by 4,436 feet. Mauna Kea is 33,465 feet tall, although 19,685 feet is beneath the ocean. The peak of Mt. Everest, at 29,029 feet, is higher above sea level. And Mt. Everest is still growing – by about 0.2 inch every year, as tectonic plates slowly shift.

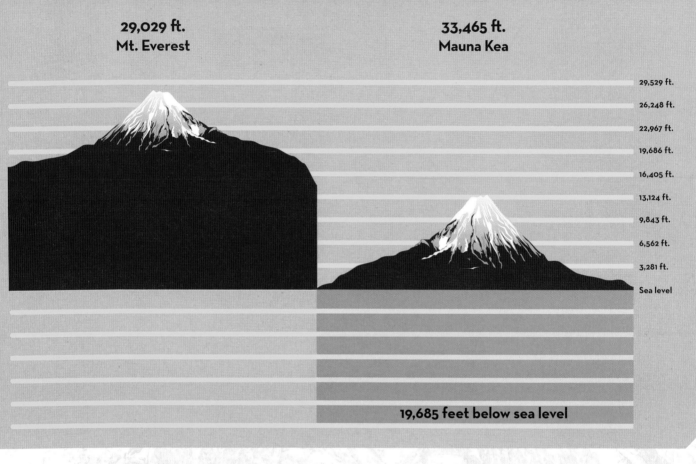

29,029 ft.
Mt. Everest

33,465 ft.
Mauna Kea

29,529 ft.
26,248 ft.
22,967 ft.
19,686 ft.
16,405 ft.
13,124 ft.
9,843 ft.
6,562 ft.
3,281 ft.
Sea level

19,685 feet below sea level

Feeling flat lately?

The Earth is not perfectly round. The planet bulges a little bit at the equator. Mt. Chimborazo, in Ecuador, is 20,565 feet high and very near the equator. That means its peak is closer to the Moon and farther from the center of the Earth than anywhere else on Earth.

Supreme forces at work

Mountains form when the Earth's surface pushes, pulls, spews, and folds. Mountains are everywhere, even under the water! The biggest mountains form when huge pieces of the Earth, called tectonic plates, push against each other and then fold upward.

Squiddly diddly do

They are only 3 inches long, but firefly squid in Japan's Toyama Bay can put on a massive light show. They have natural "glow sticks" all over their body that they flash on and off to attract a mate and confuse their enemies. Millions of the flashy squid rise to the surface of the bay in May and June.

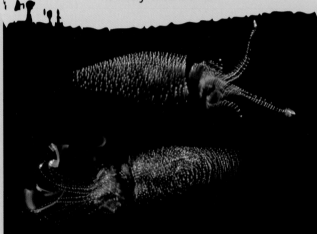

Swallow that

Mighty blue whales are the biggest animals that have ever lived on Earth. They can grow up to 110 feet long, with a heart the size of a small car, and a tongue that weighs 3 tons! But they could never swallow you up – their throats are so small, a beach ball wouldn't fit down there.

Perfect gem

The blue Logan sapphire is completely flawless and almost as big as an egg. It was found in Sri Lanka and is the largest cut sapphire on display in the world. It is set as a brooch, surrounded by diamonds. You can see it in the National Museum of Natural History in Washington, D.C.

Love nests

The male bowerbirds of New Guinea and Australia are crazy about blue. They build a beautiful nest, called a bower, on the ground, out of sticks and grass, then decorate it with all kinds of funny objects – especially blue ones! Anything goes: feathers, berries, flowers, bones, fruit, shells, bits of plastic, glass, a toothbrush or glass eye – as long as it looks neat and pretty to a female bowerbird.

BLUEST

The big blue yonder, in all its wonder

BEAR SAYS

One of my favorite watery adventures was rowing a bathtub all the way down the River Thames, in England, for charity.

Funny furry friend
This creepy greenbottle blue tarantula crawls around the deserts of Venezuela, South America.

Claim to fame
The towns of Chefchaouen, in Morocco, and Jodhpur, in India, are both nicknamed "the blue city," as many of their buildings are painted a beautiful blue. Houses on the Greek island of Santorini are famous for their domed blue roofs.

EXTREME ENDURANCE

Some of the toughest, longest, craziest challenges on Earth

SCALING 7 SUMMITS

Imagine climbing to the highest point on every continent. You need very strong legs and lungs to climb over 130,000 feet. The first person to do it was Richard Bass, in 1985. So far, only a few hundred people have managed the feat.

26,248 ft.

22,967 ft.

19,686 ft.

16,405 ft.

13,124 ft.

9,843 ft.

6,562 ft.

3,281 ft.

1. Asia Mt. Everest, Nepal 29,029 feet 2. South America Aconcagua, Argentina 22,841 feet 3. North America Denali, Alaska 20,310 feet 4. Africa Mt. Kilimanjaro, Tanzania 19,340 feet 5. Europe Mt. Elbrus, Russia 18,510 feet 6. Antarctica Vinson Massif 16,067 feet 7. Oceania Puncak Jaya (Mount Carstensz), Indonesia 16,024 feet

BRRRRRRRING IT ON!

The Iditarod Trail Sled Dog Race in Alaska is the longest dogsled race in the world. Some people do a solo version of the race, called the Iditarod Trail Invitational. It's held in winter, and contestants have to run, cycle, or ski through blizzards and subzero temperatures – without the help of furry four-footed doggy friends. You can't enter the full 1,000-mile race unless you have finished an "easy" 350-mile version first.

2,150 miles (approx.) Tour de France

Imagine peddling 1,800–2,500 miles over 21 days. That's what elite cyclists from all over the world do, trying to win the Tour de France. The course is a bit different every year, and is staged over set distances every day, but the race always winds over steep hills and mountains, with a few sprint races thrown in, and ends in Paris.

3,000 miles (approx.) Race Across America

Now imagine doing the Tour de France in about 10 days, rather than spread out over 3 weeks. Chances are you might be in the transcontinental Race Across America, from the U.S. west coast to the east coast. The route is different every year, but you'll be going pretty much nonstop for about 3,000 miles. The first race in 1982 had only four riders.

7,150 miles (approx.) Tour d'Afrique

If you need an even longer bicycle race, try the 7,450-mile Tour d'Afrique race, from Cairo to Cape Town. It starts in Egypt in the north of Africa, and ends at the very southern tip of South Africa.

Norses for courses

You have to be as strong as a Viking to finish the Norseman triathlon in Norway. First you have to swim across a freezing cold lake... then bicycle 112 miles up into the chilly hills... and then run a full 26-mile marathon, finishing on top of a mountain. Anyone who makes it to the end gets a T-shirt for their troubles!

Pretty deadly

Strawberry poison-dart frogs look good enough to eat – but you would die if you did. South American hunters use the poison from these tiny red frogs on their hunting arrows.

That's nuts

The world's reddest teeth belong to betel nut eaters. The betel nut is the seed of a palm tree. It is chewed by people in some parts of Papua New Guinea, Southeast Asia, and East Asia.

REDDEST

Colorful crimson-flushed curiosities

What's big, red, cumbersome, and the best-known symbol of London?

London's old red buses look top-heavy, but they can lean at more than 40 degrees and not tip over.

Reddy to rock

Uluru is a massive sandstone monolith in the middle of Australia. It is 5.8 miles around and 1,148 feet high – that's higher than the Eiffel Tower. It turns bright red at sunrise and sunset.

Flaming fowl

The only red shorebird in the world, the scarlet ibis lives on islands in the Caribbean Sea and parts of tropical South America. It is not born red, but starts out in life grayish white. It gets its color from the red shellfish it eats, which contain carotenoid – the same natural pigment as carrots have. So it's true: you are what you eat!

Now for my next trick...

No, he's not embarrassed. Mandrills are the world's largest monkeys and live in Africa's rain forests. They have bright-red noses and bottoms. Both ends become brighter in color when the monkey gets excited!

How shellfish!

The bright-red giant Japanese spider crab has the largest leg span of any invertebrate – 12 feet from claw to claw. Imagine the crab cake you could make! Pass the chili sauce.

BEAR SAYS

It's a myth that carrots help you see in the dark, but they are full of healthy vitamin A.

YELLOWEST

All that glitters is not gold!

BEAR SAYS

Take care around animals with yellow and black stripes. They are often venomous.

S-s-s-wampy s-s-surpri-s-se

Yellow anacondas have leopard-like markings. They lurk around swamps in South America and squeeze their prey to death before swallowing it whole. Lucky for us they are much smaller than their big green cousins – they grow to about 9.8 feet; green ones can get almost three times as long.

Eyeball this sparkly gem

The world's most expensive yellow diamond sold for $10.9 million in 2011. Called the Sun-Drop Diamond, it is the largest yellow diamond on Earth. It is as big as an eyeball.

Flight of fancy

Scientists in Canberra, Australia, have named a very rare horsefly after the pop singer Beyoncé, because it has a golden bottom. The fly is officially called Scaptia (*Plinthina*) beyonceae.

Super-powered sunbeams

Every year, the yellow Sun in our sky sends down 20,000 times more energy than people use. If we could convert more of it into electricity, then we wouldn't need to burn oil, coal, or gas – and our air would be so much cleaner.

Stamp of a multimillionaire

If you see this tiny old stamp, don't throw it away – it is worth almost $2.5 million, enough to buy 100 family cars and build a garage big enough to put them all in! Called the Treskilling Yellow, it is the world's most valuable stamp because it is the only one of its kind. It was made in Sweden in 1855. It was meant to be blue, but somehow it was printed yellow.

Greatest gold digger

The Grasberg Mine, in the Indonesian province of Papua, is the largest gold mine in the world – a hole in the ground about 2.5 miles wide. It is located high up in the mountains, near an icy glacier.

Big yellow taxis

If you are in a yellow taxi cab, you are probably in New York City. This great city has around 13,000 taxis. Some 240 million passengers make about 170 million trips in them every year. The average New York taxi travels 81,788 miles each year – equal to 3.25 times around the world. Before you are allowed to drive one, you have to go to taxi school.

Salt of the Earth

Oceans cover about 70% of the Earth's surface — and all of that water is salty, meaning we can't drink it. But how salty is it? Well, if we could remove all the salt in the ocean and spread it on the land, it would form a layer 500 feet thick. That's as tall as a 45-story building!

EXTREME OCEAN

Our big blue planet is one mighty puddle!

Long way from home

Bouvet is the most remote island in the world. You'll find it in the South Atlantic Ocean, 1,570 miles southwest of South Africa (about a two-week sail in a yacht, if you're lucky). It is covered in ice, and only moss, seals, and birds live there. In 1979, a satellite recorded a flash of light not far from Bouvet Island, which scientists think might have been caused by a nuclear explosion, or a meteor striking the Earth.

Scariest waves around

Imagine screaming down a wave as big as a 10-story building on a surfboard, with nothing but rocks and coral beneath you. Big wave surfing is one of the most dangerous sports in the world. Riders are towed out to sea by jet skis, before they tackle waves up to 90 feet high! Some of the best big waves can be found off Australia, Hawaii, California, and Portugal.

Sticking with it

People from the Marshall Islands, way out in the middle of the vast Pacific Ocean, used stick charts to navigate their canoes between islands. The stick charts were like modern maps, showing islands, wind directions, and ocean currents.

Homes under the waves

Pacific Island nations – such as Kiribati, Tuvalu, the Cook Islands, and the Marshall Islands – are in danger of disappearing under the waves because global warming is raising the sea level. Already people from the Carteret Islands in Papua New Guinea have moved to other places because their homes and crops kept being washed away by waves.

Oceans 5

There are five oceans on our planet: the Pacific, Atlantic, Indian, Southern, and Arctic. The Pacific Ocean (pictured) is the largest and deepest, while the Arctic is the smallest. Seas are small sections of the oceans, and are usually close to land. The largest seas are the South China Sea, the Caribbean Sea, and the Mediterranean Sea.

Big fish in a big pond
The biggest fish in the world could swallow you in one gulp! Whale sharks can grow almost 42 feet long, but they would never dream of eating you – they like food that is much smaller. They are very calm creatures, cruising slowly around the warm oceans. Divers sometimes hitch a ride on the back of one.

FISHY BUSINESS

Funny facts about our finny friends...

BEAR SAYS

I had a very close call once when I came face-to-face with a man-eating tiger shark in the Pacific Ocean.

Long life down under
If you were a fish and you wanted to live a long life, you would head to the bottom of the darkest, deepest oceans. Down there, fish live longer than we do. Some rockfish, living about 9,800 feet below the ocean surface, are more than 200 years old! Most of them live in the Pacific Ocean.

Tiny fish in a tiny puddle

The world's smallest fish is also the world's smallest animal with a backbone. This tiny see-through carp is only 0.3 inch long and lives in swamps in Sumatra and Borneo. It doesn't mind a drought because it can live in the tiniest puddles. These fish are so small you could hide one under your fingernail!

Flashy splashy

Lake Malawi in Africa contains more fish species than any other lake on Earth – including more than 300 different types of these colorful cichlid fish.

Tetra packs it in

Blind Mexican tetra fish that live in caves used to have eyes, but because they have spent the last million or so years in the dark, their skin has grown over their peepers. Mysteriously, they avoid bumping into other fish. No one really understands why.

I thought you were dead!

Everyone thought the coelacanth fish had died out 65 million years ago, until a live one turned up off the coast of South Africa in 1938! The fish has been around since before dinosaurs roamed the Earth.

Playing with rays

The huge stingrays at Stingray City on the Cayman Islands in the Caribbean are so tame they will come right up to you. They don't actually "sting," but they do have a pointy barb under their tail that they use for protection.

CONGO CRAZY

Africa's biggest rain forest and river are home to some amazing people, plants, and animals

Found only in the Congo...

Bonobo apes
Peace-loving bonobo apes are our closest relatives, sharing over 98% of our DNA. In bonobo families, the females are in charge.

Okapi
What has a brown body like a horse, legs like a zebra, a tongue like a giraffe – and is found nowhere else on Earth? Why, the okapi of course! It is a close cousin of the giraffe – the males even have short, hair-covered horns like giraffes. Okapi are hard to spot in the forest as their crazy coloring gives them excellent forest camouflage.

Congo peacock
The elusive Congo peacock is hard to find. It is at risk of extinction.

Forest people
Traditional tribes in the forest include the Mbuti and Mbenga people, who are very short – men are often less than 5 feet tall. Their way of life is in danger because other people are chopping their forest down.

Deadly work
Would you climb 100 feet up a tree to gather honey from a hive full of angry bees? The very bravest Mbuti men do, because their tribe loves honey. A bird called the greater honeyguide shows them where the beehives are.

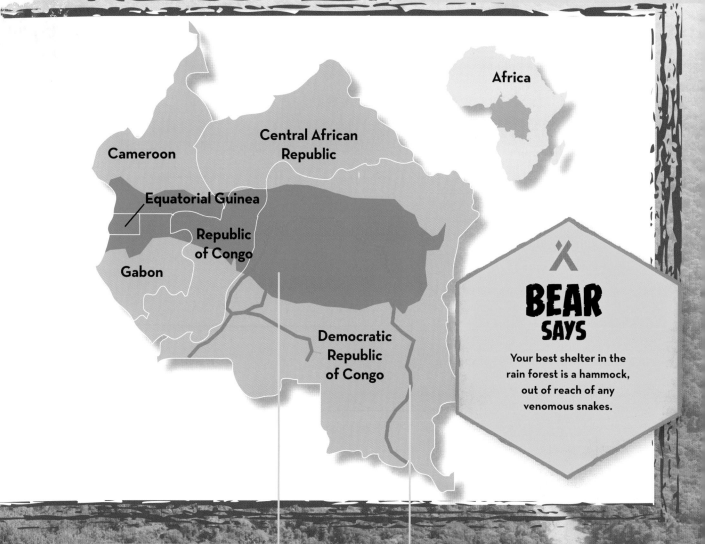

Africa

Cameroon

Central African Republic

Equatorial Guinea

Republic of Congo

Gabon

Democratic Republic of Congo

BEAR SAYS

Your best shelter in the rain forest is a hammock, out of reach of any venomous snakes.

Congo Rain Forest

- This is the world's second biggest rain forest, after the Amazon.
- It is home to 11,000 plant species, 1,150 bird species, 450 mammal species, 300 reptile species, and 200 amphibian species.
- In some parts, the forest is so thick that the only way to travel through it is by boat, along the Congo River – and modern explorers haven't been able to get in there.
- Each year, more forest is being chopped down because of logging and mining, and to make room for growing crops and building villages.
- Many forest animals – like gorillas – are being killed and eaten by hungry people as "bush meat." This leaves many species at risk of extinction.

Congo River

- The Congo River is the world's deepest river: some stretches are over 640 feet deep.
- By volume of water, the Congo River is Africa's largest river – even though it is not as long as Africa's longest river, the Nile. The Congo is 2,900 miles long, while the Nile is 4,130 miles long.
- The river is home to almost 700 different fish species.
- It crosses the equator twice, and is up to 15 miles wide.
- The river's falls and rapids have as much power as all the rivers and falls in the US put together. Some rapids are so fast and powerful they are too dangerous to cross – such as the 75-mile-long "Gates of Hell."

Monster tales

Since ancient times, people around the world have been seeing different kinds of monsters – from the black, serpent-like pinatubo of the Philippines, the ogopogo of Canada, the mysterious mokèlé-mbèmbé and the emela-ntouka of Africa, to the bunyips of outback Australia. The most famous is Scotland's Loch Ness Monster, nicknamed "Nessie," which lives in a large sea lake.

Psst, can you keep a SECRET?

Wast Water lake, in the UK, has a secret "gnome garden" at the bottom of it. In 2005, police removed the gnomes because they were planted very deep and some divers died trying to find them – but other divers keep putting more gnomes back in the lake. Divers say there are about 40 gnomes... and growing.

Pass the pepper please...

The world's largest dried salt lake is Salar de Uyuni, high up in the Andes Mountains in Bolivia (pictured). It covers 4,086 sqare miles, and the salt in some parts is over 33 feet thick. When it rains, the lake is covered in water and becomes the world's largest natural mirror! Pink flamingos breed here.

Russian record-breaker

The world's largest, deepest, and oldest freshwater lake is Lake Baikal in Siberia. It holds 20% of the planet's unfrozen fresh water. In winter, it freezes into a great big ice block.

BEAR SAYS

The worst creatures you could share the water with would be a hungry school of piranhas. They live throughout the Amazon River basin, so be careful swimming there!

LOTS OF LOVELY LAKES

Planet Earth has over 304 million lakes – that's plenty of room to make a splash!

World's 5 BIGGEST lakes

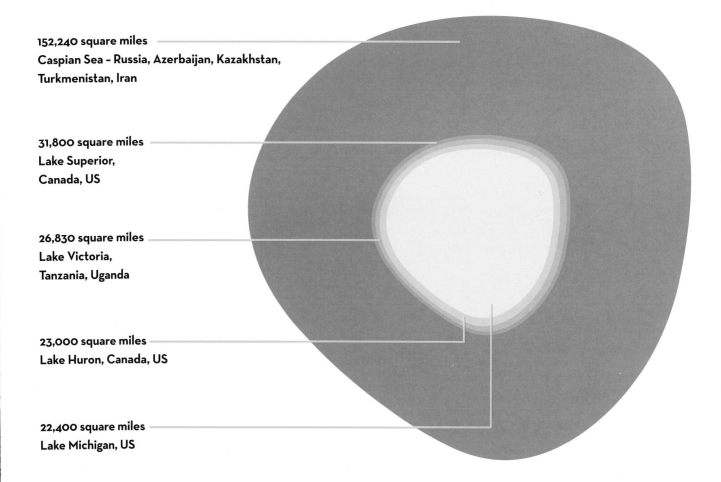

152,240 square miles
Caspian Sea – Russia, Azerbaijan, Kazakhstan, Turkmenistan, Iran

31,800 square miles
Lake Superior, Canada, US

26,830 square miles
Lake Victoria, Tanzania, Uganda

23,000 square miles
Lake Huron, Canada, US

22,400 square miles
Lake Michigan, US

The Caspian Sea is considered a lake because it is enclosed all around by land. The next four largest lakes would easily fit inside it – as well as the next four largest after that: Lake Aral (Kazakhstan, Uzbekistan), Lake Tanganyika (Tanzania, Congo), Lake Baikal (Russia), and Great Bear (Canada).

TREASURE ISLANDS

Ahoy there! I spy sanctuaries in the sea...

BEAR SAYS

If you are shipwrecked on a desert island, find water, build shelter, and start a campfire.

The land that time forgot

The Galápagos Islands, off the coast of South America in the Pacific Ocean, are a most unusual spot. Almost 9,000 different species of animals live here. Because they have been isolated from the mainland for millions of years, many of the animals are found nowhere else in the world – for example, the Galápagos penguin – the only penguin that lives on the equator.

Far, far away

If you want to get away from it all, try Tristan da Cunha, in the southern Atlantic Ocean. The island is 1,750 miles from anywhere else, making it the most remote inhabited island in the world. There's one radio station and 262 people.

TRISTAN DA CUNHA
SOUTH ATLANTIC

Unreal islands

The Middle Eastern desert country of Dubai is home to the largest artificial islands in the world. The "Palm Islands" are built in the shape of palm trees, from sand dredged from the bottom of the ocean, and are about 3 miles across. There is also a group of islands called "The World," which looks like a map of the world.

Small and light

The smallest inhabitable island in the world is Bishop Rock, off the UK coast. It is about 151 feet long and 52 feet wide and is almost completely covered by a lighthouse. Many years ago criminals were sent to the island to die.

BEAR SAYS

Spices such as cloves and cinnamon kill microbes in food, keeping it fresher.

Hot and spicy

The Maluku and Banda Islands in Indonesia are the spiciest islands in the world. They were once called the Spice Islands because rare spices such as nutmeg, mace, and cloves grew there. Banda was once the only place in the world where nutmeg grew. In the 1600s nutmeg was more valuable than gold!

55

Big bangs

A 2009 earthquake in L'Aquila, Italy (pictured), killed 308 people. The biggest earthquake ever recorded shook the whole Earth for days. The 9.5 magnitude earthquake in Valdivia, Chile, on May 22, 1960, killed more than 1,600 people and caused a huge ocean wave, called a tsunami, that then killed many more people in faraway Hawaii, Japan, and the Philippines.

Puzzle it out

The outer layer of our Earth is called the crust. But it's not in one piece. Instead it's made up of lots of smaller pieces, like a jigsaw puzzle. And all those separate pieces, called tectonic plates, are constantly moving and bumping against each other. Earthquakes occur when two of these plates that are touching suddenly move. The power of an earthquake is called its magnitude, and is measured out of 10. Volcanoes are also often found around the edges of tectonic plates, where the Earth's crust is thinner.

Hi there, neighbor!

In California, the Pacific and North American tectonic plates slide past each other at 2 inches every year, along the San Andreas Fault. That's about as fast as your fingernails grow. The city of Los Angeles is on one plate, and the city of San Francisco is on the other. Even though they are now 348 miles apart, they'll slide past each other in about 15 million years.

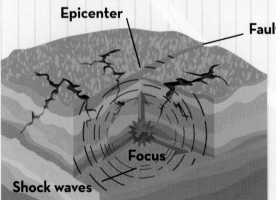

Epicenter

Fault line

Focus

Shock waves

Shaking all over

About 1.5 million earthquakes shake the world each year. That is almost three earthquakes every minute! Thankfully, most are so small you can't feel them.

SHAKY PLANET

Solid earth isn't always as solid as we hope...

BEAR SAYS

If you're by the sea during an earthquake, race for higher ground in case of a tsunami.

Hell's furnace

If you could fly over Nyiragongo volcano in the Democratic Republic of Congo, Africa, and look into its crater, you would see an amazing light show. The brilliant show is caused by the most violent molten lava lake in the world, which spits and bubbles and glows bright orange. The lava is coming from deep under the ground.

Ring of Fire

The Pacific Ring of Fire is the world's most volcanic area. It is a 25,000-mile horseshoe of 452 volcanoes and constant earthquakes, around the edges of the Pacific Ocean, where lots of tectonic plates meet. More than 90% of all the world's earthquakes happen here. You'll also find half the world's volcanoes here.

10 most venomous snakes...

...and they are all from Australia, the Deadly Snake Capital of the Universe!

However, only about three or four people a year die from snake bites in Australia.
1. Inland taipan (it has enough venom to kill about 100 people) 2. Eastern brown snake
3. Coastal taipan 4. Tiger snake 5. Western tiger snake 6. Beaked sea snake
7. Black tiger snake 8. Death adder 9. Gwardar 10. Spotted brown snake

SLITHERIEST

Sssnooping into the sssecret world of sssnakesss...

They've got a crush on you

The world's largest snake, the green anaconda, can grow to 25 feet long. It is not quite as long as the world's longest snake, the reticulated python, but the green anaconda is fatter and up to twice as heavy, weighing up to a whopping 550 pounds. Both snakes get their food by wrapping themselves around an animal and crushing it to death. They then swallow it whole, headfirst, so the legs go down smoothly. They can easily open out their jaws to gobble up animals much wider than themselves – even a deer with big antlers... and even YOU!

How charming

In the Indian subcontinent and northern Africa, snake charmers play music to snakes to try to hypnotize them. Not something you should try at home!

BEAR SAYS

If you're bitten by a snake, stay calm, keep movement to a minimum – and get help.

Fleet without feet

You can't outrun a black mamba, thought to be the world's quickest snake. It can slither at up to 12 mph. It is also Africa's longest venomous snake.

A real killer

It is thought that each year about 14,000 people in southern Asia, 11,000 people in India, and many people in Africa die after being bitten by venomous snakes such as cobras and vipers. This is not because these snakes are actually the most venomous, but because the people can't get medical help quickly enough.

Light fantastic

They say lightning doesn't strike twice – but in Venezuela, lightning strikes thousands of times a night! For 10 hours a night, about 150 nights a year, the angry skies hurl up to 280 lightning bolts an hour over big, mysterious Lake Maracaibo. This amazing "catatumbo lightning" can be seen up to 250 miles away.

Flash figures

No wonder they hurt so much! The temperature of a lightning bolt can reach 55,000°F – five times hotter than the Sun's surface. Lightning strikes the ground about 8 million times a day – about 100 times every second! Lots more lightning flashes up in the clouds, without ever hitting the ground.

Seven times lucky

American national park ranger Roy Sullivan was hit by lightning seven times between 1942 and 1977 – and survived them all.

EXTREME WEATHER

Nature's fury unleashed

BEAR SAYS

The first priority of survival is to find or build protection from the weather.

Rain, rain, go away

Lloró in Colombia is the wettest place on Earth. It gets an amazing 524 inches of rain every year! It's not the wettest place on record, though. Back in 1860–61, Cherrapunji in India received nearly double that amount: 1,042 inches.

It never rains in Arizona

At least it rarely rains in Yuma, Arizona. This small city is in the middle of a desert and is the sunniest place in the world. Out of 4,456 hours of daylight every year, the Sun shines for 4,174 hours – or about 94% of the time!

Fishiest thunderstorms

Almost every year, in May or June, a storm rolls through the town of Yoro, in Honduras. There is lightning, thunder, and heavy rain for two hours. Once it is over, hundreds of living fish are found flopping around on the ground. No one knows for certain how they get there. The town holds the Festival of the Rain of Fishes (*Festival de la Lluvia de Peces*) to celebrate.

Waves of destruction

The December 26, 2004 tsunami was the deadliest and most destructive tsunami ever recorded. A massive earthquake, with the same power as 23,000 atomic bombs, shook the Indian Ocean, creating a huge tidal wave that slammed into 12 countries, including Indonesia, Sri Lanka, India, Thailand and the Maldives. The tsunami killed more than 226,000 people and left millions homeless. Tsunamis are most common in the Pacific Ocean, in countries on the Pacific "Ring of Fire," which have lots of volcanoes and earthquakes. Tsunami is a Japanese word meaning "harbor wave."

Have a heart, or three
Cuttlefish have the greenest blood of any animal. They also have three hearts to pump that blood around their body!

Gem of a stone
The most popular green gemstone is the emerald. The largest emerald ever found is as big as a watermelon – called the Teodora, from Brazil! It is valued at over $1 million.

Turning green
If you find yourself eating green sausages, you might be at a St. Patrick's Day festival. That's when millions of Irish people all around the world eat green food, drink green drinks, and wear green clothes to celebrate St. Patrick arriving in Ireland. Held on March 17, St. Patrick's Day is celebrated in more countries than any other national day.

Mossiest mammal
Sloths live in the jungles of South America and move very s-l-o-w-l-y. They move so slowly that algae grows on them, turning their fur green.

Happy place

One of the "greenest" countries in the world is Bhutan, high up in the Himalayas. About 70% of Bhutan is covered in thick green forest, and the country is also very good at protecting its environment. It banned plastic bags and cigarettes because they make people unhappy. The country measures its success by its "Gross National Happiness!"

GREENEST

The great green globe in all its glory

White wash

Greenland isn't actually green. Much of it is thick white ice!

Whoa, boa

Perhaps the greenest snake is the emerald tree boa. This slithery serpent lives in the rain forests of South America and can hide very well in the lush green trees, where it waits for small animals to come along. Then it squeezes them to death before swallowing them.

BIRD BRAINS

Flighty facts from the featheriest kingdom

Eggs-agerated egg-stremes

Growing up to 9 feet tall, the African ostrich is the world's largest bird. It also lays the world's largest eggs, which can weigh a whopping 3 pounds each – with about the same volume as 24 chicken eggs! The world's smallest bird is the tiny bee hummingbird, from Cuba. People often mistake it for an insect! You could put 4,700 of its pea-sized eggs inside just one ostrich egg.

Showiest bird

Male peafowl, called peacocks, use their beautiful feathers to dazzle the females. Their tails are so large they can't fly very well, but they do look handsome!

Sharp shooters

An eagle soaring high in the air can spot a rabbit on the ground 1 mile away. It has especially large eyes and special retinas that let it see very sharply straight ahead, and also to the side. It can then swoop down on its unsuspecting prey at up to 124 mph.

Cash for quetzals

Quetzals are beautiful, colorful birds that live in South America. They grow such lengthy tails, up to 3 feet long, that they can't take off out of trees properly, because their tail sometimes gets caught on branches. The people of Guatemala love their quetzals so much they named their money after them.

Only half asleep

When flamingos go to sleep, they do so one side at a time. When they want to have a snooze, they lift one leg up and let that side go to sleep. When they want to rest the other side, they swap legs. Some flamingos eat certain algae that contain a chemical that turns them the brightest pink.

Extreme endurance

The emperor penguin is the world's biggest penguin. It lives in just about the harshest environment on Earth. These plucky birds waddle up to 75 miles across snow and ice to get to their breeding grounds. After mom has laid her egg, dad puts it on his feet, rests his fat, feathery belly on top to keep it warm, then stands shivering with thousands of other dads in the freezing wind and snow for two months while mom takes to the ocean to feed. Mom finally comes back and vomits up food for the chick that has hatched under dad's tummy. They then take turns raising the young chick.

Monster's flesh breath

Most people try to do something about their bad breath, but some animals want it as awful as possible! Komodo dragons, from Indonesia, have toxic bacteria in their mouth, which smells foul. They also leave rotting flesh in their teeth, which smells even fouler. All that badness in their mouths helps kill their prey when they chomp into it.

Dead giveaway

Do you like the smell of rotting flesh? Some insects do, and that's why they love a giant flower called the titan arum, or corpse flower. It smells like an old dead body. The insects visit the flower and help pollinate the plant. The corpse flower is the biggest flower in the world – up to 10 feet high. It doesn't bloom very often – maybe only once every few years – and when it does flower, the stinky thing only lasts for about three days. It grows on the Indonesian island of Sumatra.

BEAR SAYS

Our sense of smell is a key survival tool. If food or water smells bad, it probably is!

SMELLIEST

Some of the stinkiest things on Earth!

Heaven and hell

Durian is a tropical fruit that is said to "taste like heaven and smell like hell." Some people say it smells like sewage or vomit. The odor is so foul, durian is banned on public transportation in most of Southeast Asia, where it grows. It does, however, taste delicious!

Curb your curd

In France, smelly cheese is banned on public transportation. Époisses de Bourgogne, said to be the world's stinkiest cheese, is a no-no on buses and trains in Paris.

Let's skip dinner...

Fresh fish is healthy and delicious. But if kept too long, it turns really nasty.

Surströmming, from Sweden, is canned fermented Baltic herring. The fermenting herrings can sometimes make the cans buckle. The cans are banned on airlines because they might blow up! Most people eat it outside because of its hideous pong.

Hákarl, from Iceland, is the fermented flesh of a shark that has been buried in the ground for three months, and then dried for six months before it is eaten.

Narezushi is a Japanese delicacy made from salted fish that is fermented with rice for four years.

Shoot a hole in one

The world's deadliest golf course is thought to be on the border of North and South Korea, at a United Nations military post called Camp Bonifas. The golf course green has minefields on three sides. A golf ball one person hit exploded a land mine – kabooom!

Which bean slays witch

People accused of being witches in Nigeria had to eat poisonous calabar beans in an "ordeal by bean." Most then died a horrible death. The ordeal is now banned – but the beans still grow... so whatever you do, don't eat them!

DEFINITELY DEADLY

Stay away from these things!

This big bird is a real ripper

Cassowaries can't fly, but these big birds can give you a deadly kick. Their feet have three toes – the middle one is long, knife-like and able to rip you open. A fast runner, this scary-looking bird can jump almost 6.6 feet straight into the air. Luckily it is quite shy. It lives in New Guinea and northern Australia.

Death Road

The North Yungas Road in Bolivia is known as the Road of Death, or El Camino de la Muerte, because about 300 people die on it every year. It is probably the most dangerous road in the world. It is only 10 feet wide – and there are no safety rails between the road and a 1,830-foot drop to the valley below.

BEAR SAYS

The closest I've come to death was when I broke my back skydiving in southern Africa. The many months of recovery taught me to live life boldly and with gratitude.

Annoying little killers

They don't have big teeth or sharp claws, but tiny mosquitoes are the deadliest insect or animal in the world. That's because they drink our blood, and at the same time they can pass on deadly diseases such as malaria and yellow fever. They may have killed as many as 46 billion people – that's half the number of people who have ever lived!

Lethal to a point

The golden poison arrow frog is only 2 inches long, but it contains enough venom to kill 10 adults. That's why this most deadly frog is used by South American tribes to make their poison hunting darts.

JUNGLE JUMBOS

The strangest facts about the most curious critters

Pet for the pot
Some people like guinea pigs as pets – other people like them with potatoes! Guinea pigs are a popular food in Peru and Bolivia because they are tasty, high in protein, and don't need much room to be raised in.

EGG with LEGS
Balut is known as the "treat with feet," and is a very popular street food in the Philippines. It is a duck or chicken egg that has been buried in the ground for a few weeks, so that the baby bird inside starts to form. The egg is then soft-boiled – and the feathery insides eaten with a spoon!

BEAR SAYS
One of the worst things I've eaten was a rhino beetle. It was crunchy, but I choked it down!

Ant that strange?
In the Santander region of Colombia, giant ants are a popular snack. The heads, legs, and wings are chopped off, then the ants are salted and fried. They taste smoky, and crackle when you crunch on them.

It's really good grub

You can find plump white witchetty grubs in the trunks and roots of trees in central Australia. Local Aborigines snack on them, either raw or cooked, and some restaurants even serve them as delicacies. When cooked, they taste a little bit like chicken with peanut sauce!

Dinner with a bite

Some restaurants in Vietnam serve up cobra. You can try the still-beating heart as an appetizer, before enjoying cobra soup, cobra spring rolls, and barbecued cobra.

Hopping out for dinner

If people in Dominica, in the Caribbean, couldn't find mountain chickens, they used to enjoy eating the next best thing – "mountain chicken frogs." One of the biggest frogs in the world, they can weigh up to 2.2 pounds. But all that fine dining means the frogs are now becoming rare.

BEAR SAYS

I once ate undigested apples I found in a bear poop. That's not a recipe you should ever try!

71

RAIN FORESTS OF THE SEA

Coral reefs are home to more plant and animal species than anywhere else on Earth, except rain forests. They take up an area half the size of France, yet hold a quarter of all marine life.

Old beauties

Despite their size, coral reefs grow very, very slowly – only about 1.2 inches every year. Some coral reefs are more than 50 million years old!

Big brain in the drain

It's the world's biggest brain, but it is not very smart. In Kelleston Drain, off the coast of Tobago in the Caribbean, a brain coral measuring 10 feet by 16 feet sits around thinking about not much at all. It's called brain coral because it is shaped like a huge piece of gray matter.

Beauty from destruction

In the Solomon Islands, sunken wrecks of boats and tanks from World War II are slowly being taken over by coral reefs. You can dive down and see the rusty machines covered in corals, that are now home to thousands of colorful fish.

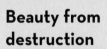

BEAR SAYS

Our coral reefs are in deadly danger from rising sea temperatures and water pollution.

Greatest reef ever

Australia's Great Barrier Reef, off the coast of Queensland, is the largest living structure on Earth. If you were up in the International Space Station, you could easily see it. The reef is more than 1,600 miles long. That's greater than the distance between London and Moscow!

The Great Barrier Reef
- is made up of 2,900 individual reefs and 900 islands
- covers 86 million acres – about the same size as Japan.

It is home to:

30	1,500	350	6
species of whales, dolphins, and porpoises	fish species	coral species	sea turtle species

Sea-loving "jumbos"
The Great Barrier Reef has one of the world's largest colonies of dugongs. More related to elephants than dolphins, peaceful dugongs are also called "sea cows" or "sea camels."

Animal, mineral, or vegetable?
Coral reefs are made up of really tiny animals called polyps. The wild colors that you see in coral reefs come from the billions of algae that live in the polyps. The algae also hold all the tiny polyps together so they eventually form big reefs.

WEB SITES

A yarn or two about nature's best spinners

Pleased to meet you
The happy face spider, from Hawaii, may look like the friendliest spider in the world, but it really developed its special markings as a camouflage to stop birds eating it.

Come to momma!
The most motherly spider in the world must be the wolf spider. The female carries her eggs with her until the spiderlings hatch. Then they all hop onto mom's back and ride around for a couple of weeks.

Quite a bite
The most venomous spider in the world is the Brazilian wandering spider. It has enough venom to kill 180 mice.

Munching on spiders

Imagine being so hungry you could eat a big, black hairy spider. There was a time when people in Cambodia were so hungry that they caught tarantulas in the jungle, then fried them whole – fangs and all! – until nice and crunchy, but still a bit soft in the middle. Now people visit the town of Skuon to try them.

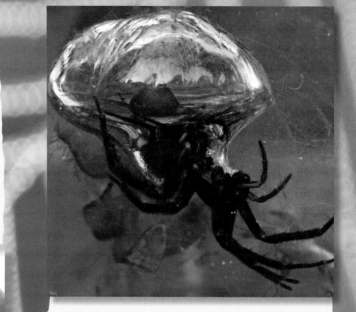

Spider diver

The diving bell spider can stay under water all day by creating a bubble of air in a silk sack. The bubble can draw oxygen from the surrounding water, like gills in a fish, but the spider needs to race up to the surface of the water every day to grab a large gulp of fresh air. It catches little fish instead of flies!

By golly, it's enormous!

The biggest spider in the world is the goliath bird eater, which terrorizes wildlife in South America's jungles. An early European explorer saw one eating a hummingbird, hence its name. Its leg span can be up to 11 inches – nearly as long as a ruler. Never fear, it can't see very well. Just as well!

Animal magnetism

Sea turtles could be the oceans' greatest navigators. They hatch from eggs their mom buried in the sand on beaches around the world. After they are born, they travel up to 3,000 miles across the oceans in search of food and friendship. But when they are ready to lay their own eggs, the sea turtles swim back to the same beach they were born on! Scientists think the turtles have magnetic crystals in their brains and use the Earth's magnetism and an inbuilt map to navigate.

MAKING SENSE

The super senses of the animal kingdom

BEAR SAYS

Humans rely heavily on their sight, but in the wild remember to use your other senses, too.

TASTE

Touchy tasty

A catfish doesn't even need to eat something to know whether it tastes good or not. The fish has "whiskers" around its mouth, which "taste" things they touch. The catfish also has very sensitive skin that can "smell" chemicals in the water!

TOUCH

Blind mole's star attraction

It may look weird, but the star-nosed mole uses the 22 little "fingers" on its nose to feel its way around its dark and wet underground home. It is almost blind, so it "sees" with its nose. The mole's pink starry nose also lets it quickly decide whether something it touches is tasty, even underwater. It can find and eat food faster than any other animal.

Sounding out a scene

Some animals, such as bats, use sounds to "see" where they are going. They make a noise, such as a click, and listen for it to echo off whatever is around it. Their brains then create a scene from the sounds, just like our brains do from what our eyes see. This is called echolocation. A few blind people have also worked out how to use echolocation to "see" – some can even ride bicycles and go bush walking!

SOUND

SMELL

Sensational sniffers

Bears have a better sense of smell than any other land animal. They use it to find food, a partner, and to help them stay away from danger. When polar bears are hunting, they can smell a seal under 3 feet of ice, from more than 0.6 miles away.

Keeping eyes on the prize

Imagine being able to spot a rabbit sitting in the grass from 1 mile away! Eagles and other birds of prey can do this as they soar through the air. They then swoop down at up to 124 mph, while keeping their target in focus all the way.

SIGHT

Hear are some great ears

Owls have amazing hearing. They can hear a mouse walking 75 feet away! Dolphins use their ears to hear – but they also use their jaw. Sounds make their jaw vibrate, and these vibrations reach their inner ear. Scientists think elephants can feel sound through their trunk and feet, as well as through their great big flappy ears.

43500 MI

Tern for the better

Arctic terns are the world's greatest commuters. Every year, these tiny birds fly from Greenland and Iceland, up near the North Pole, to feed at the very bottom of the world, in the Antarctic. They fly about 43,500 miles every year – that's almost twice around the world!

1865 MI

It's a long way home

Could you find your way back to your front door if you had just spent five years traveling halfway around the world? Pacific salmon can! The salmon leave the rivers where they are born, to live in the Pacific Ocean for four or five years, before they return to the same river to lay eggs. Amazingly, they don't simply return to the same river, they also return to the exact spot on the river in which they were born.

3700 MI

Caribou come through

Every year, huge herds of reindeer, also called caribou, charge across the Arctic areas of Canada in search of food and to avoid wolves. Some groups travel 3,700 miles a year – farther than any other land mammal.

Hooves of thunder

The largest animal migration on Earth occurs on the Serengeti plains in Africa, when more than 2 million wildebeest and zebras leave Tanzania for the lush green grass of the Masai Mara region of neighboring Kenya in March. About 250,000 animals will die on the way – some of them chomped by hungry crocodiles waiting for them to cross the Mara River.

3 7 0 0 0 0 0 MI

Gliding to the Moon

An albatross might fly more than 10,000 miles to deliver one meal to its chick. But it doesn't get too tired. Its huge wingspan – up to 11 feet – means it can glide for hours without flapping. By the time it is 50 years old, an albatross will have flown at least 3.7 million miles. The average distance between the Earth and the Moon is 238,857 miles ... so this means an albatross could have flown to the Moon and back eight times, hardly flapping its wings!

ON THE MOVE

A flurry of feet, fins, hooves, and feathers: globe-trotting critters

Great red tide

Christmas Island, in the Indian Ocean, is home to 1,400 people and 50 million red crabs! You don't see them much, but once a year the crabs leave their burrows and head for the sea to lay their eggs – up to 100,000 at a time. This huge migration covers the island in a moving red carpet. Then all the red crabs and their babies move back inland again!

🏔
BEAR SAYS

In 2011, Jean Béliveau completed a 47,000-mile walk around the world.

Sealed in a seal

Next time you get served something you're not keen on, be thankful you're not sitting down for dinner in Greenland: you might be given kiviak. These are seabirds called auks that are preserved by being put – unplucked – inside a gutted seal that is then buried under rocks. After a few months the seal is dug up. You eat the fermented auks by pulling off the bird's head and eating the insides.

Slimy escape artist

Hagfish slip out of danger by producing a hideous slimy gel that clogs their attacker's gills, giving them time to wriggle away. Hagfish can produce enough slime to turn a bucket of water to gel in minutes. They can also tie themselves into a knot.

It's a mitey planet

You might think you are clean, but your body is crawling with tiny creatures so small you can't even see them. There are more than 5,000 creatures living on every 0.2 square inches of your body! Your skin is home to more critters than there are people on the planet.

YUCKIEST

Don't look now – these things are really disgusting!

Froggy smoothie

Big wrinkly frogs from Lake Titicaca in Peru are unique and under threat. The funny folds in their skin absorb oxygen from the water, letting them breathe underwater. But that's not why they are in trouble. Locals think they are good for their health. They use a blender to turn them into soup and then drink them!

Waste of a life

Imagine living your WHOLE LIFE up to your knees in poop! Dung beetles couldn't be happier than when they have lots of fresh animal manure to live in. They eat some of it, and they lay eggs on the rest then bury it. On a good day, a dung beetle can bury 250 times its own weight in dung.

BEAR SAYS

I've eaten frogs in the wild, but many species are endangered – so don't do it at home!

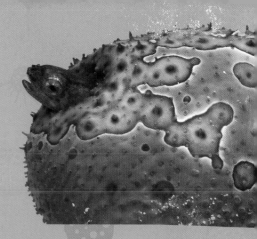

Some like it hot

Giant tube worms like to bed down among toxic chemicals, boiling temperatures, and extreme pressure, 8,200 feet below the surface of the ocean. The worms live in hard tubes right next to volcanic vents on the ocean floor and feast on bacteria.

When home is a real bummer

Living inside another animal's bottom might seem like the worst home in the world, but pearlfish, which live along Australia's Great Barrier Reef, seem to find it quite all right. The pearlfish makes its home inside a sea cucumber's bum because it's a good spot to hide from predators.

Dig right in

Human botflies like to make their home right under your skin! The flies lay their eggs on you and when the eggs hatch the maggots burrow under your skin and feed on your flesh. They are mainly found in Central and South America.

Branching out

You have to wonder if killifish, which live in the mangrove swamps of Belize and in Florida, really think they are birds. The strange fish spend a few months every year breathing air and living in trees, when the muddy pools they normally swim in dry up.

Ant antics

Ants might have the busiest and biggest homes in the world. One massive colony of ants on the Mediterranean coast is more than 3,700 miles long and contains billions and billions of ants.

Bear with us...
Microscopic water bears can live anywhere and are probably the hardiest animals on the planet. They like to live in moist moss – but if the moss dries out they'll happily go to sleep until the moss becomes wet again. Some water bears sleeping in dried moss that had been in a museum for 100 years woke up when the moss was moistened! They'll also survive being boiled, frozen, shot into space, irradiated, poisoned, and suffocated.

ANIMAL ABODES

Some critters live in the most curious places

BEAR SAYS

One of the best places I've bedded down has to be inside a snow hole in the icy Arctic.

The high life
High up in the sky live tiny things. Scientists have found bacteria, fungi, and viruses living up to 11 miles above the Earth. That's twice as high as the bar-headed goose can fly (see page 93). But you wouldn't want to be flying around with them. Some of these bugs can kill you!

PLANT PLANET

Wonders of the plant world

Pretty large, in general

The largest tree in the world is General Sherman, a giant sequoia in California. It is not the tallest or the widest tree, but it has the most volume of wood in it. In northern California, there are coast redwoods so large that roads have been built right through their trunks!

Humungous fungus

A giant honey mushroom in Oregon covers an area of 3.4 square miles, making it the largest single living thing by area. It's about the size of 2,200 soccer fields.

VIP killer

One tasty-looking death cap mushroom contains enough poison to kill a grown-up. Some people accidentally eat it, because it looks like other, safe mushrooms. Fatal mistake! Scientists think it is responsible for most mushroom poisonings in the world. Native to Europe and Asia, the mushroom has killed popes, Roman emperors, and royalty.

GENERAL SHERMAN

Mighty weighty

The heaviest single living thing on Earth is a forest of 47,000 aspen trees in Utah. The trees, which weigh 6,000 tons, are counted as one thing because they share a root system and are all genetically the same.

Grow with the flow

Giant kelp forests in the ocean (pictured) are thought to be the world's fastest-growing plants. The leaves can grow more than 20 inches every day! You could swim 200 feet straight down and you would still not find their roots.

Pitcher this!

Pitcher plants are shaped like a jug with a lid on top. These sly incognito carnivores lure little insects into the jug with tasty nectar on their rim. Then the lid snaps shut and the insect is slowly digested. One pitcher plant is as big as a soccer ball and quite happily gobbles up mice and rats!

Forest frolics

Rhubarb is a plant that many people cook for dessert, but in Chile it is home to the world's smallest deer, the pudú, which lives among giant rhubarb. These rhubarb forests are a strange world in miniature, because the tiny pudú, which are only about knee-high, are often hunted by little wild cats called kodkod, the size of kittens.

Hey, handsome!

The male proboscis monkey has the biggest, funniest nose. And a big pot belly full of windy gas from all the leaves, seeds, and fruit he gobbles.

Deep-sea frills

The frilled shark is the frilliest shark ever. A living fossil, it is one of the oldest species on Earth – it's been around for up to 100 million years. Frilled sharks are very rarely seen as they live in very deep, dark water. They look more like an eel or a real-life sea serpent than a shark, but their big, wide grinning mouths are full of about 300 needle-sharp hooked teeth.

Skinny socialites

Wrinkly and bucktoothed, little naked mole rats live in large underground colonies in the deserts of eastern Africa. Led by a single female queen, these highly social creatures live and work together, building very long and complex burrows. They can travel backward as quickly as they can go forward – and strangely, their skin doesn't feel pain. They can live for up to 30 years – about 10 times longer than other rats! Scientists are fascinated by these animals as they never get cancer.

Two-legged lizard wizard

The little Mexican mole lizard, or ajolote, isn't really a lizard at all, although it is a close lizard relative. It looks more like a worm – except for its two lizard-like legs, right up near its head. It lives underground in little tunnels, using its claws to shuffle through soil and find yummy grubs and insects to eat.

KOOKY CRITTERS

The most curious creatures around...

BEAR SAYS

Just like these animals, in the wild you must use the tools you have and trust your skills.

Turbo powered

Unlike other fish, the fist-sized psychedelic frogfish doesn't have scales. Instead, it has fleshy, flabby skin. Also, unlike other fish, it can't swim. It bounces around the sea floor, on its blobby foot-like fins. It also uses jet propulsion to spurt about all over the place, by shooting water through its gills. This curiosity was only discovered in 2008.

Aye yay yay!

The aye-aye is the world's largest – and probably freakiest – nocturnal primate. It lives only on the island of Madagascar, high up in trees. It taps its long, skinny middle finger on trees, looking for tasty grubs, which it then scoops out with its finger. Aye-ayes are dying out because local people kill them, thinking they bring bad luck.

Those brave crocodile men

Young men of the Sepik River's Kaningara tribe show their bravery and manhood by being scarred with a crocodile tattoo. Deep wounds are cut into their bodies, in the pattern of crocodile scales. These wounds are rubbed with mud, oil, and ashes to turn them into big scars, which they will have forever. The young men learn secret stories during this painful ordeal.

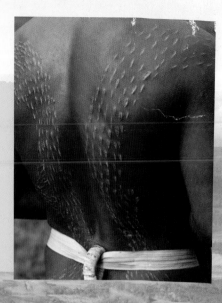

1,000 NEW SPECIES
in 10 years!

From 1998 to 2008, scientists studying PNG found:

218
new plants

580
new invertebrates

134
new amphibians

43
new reptiles

71
new fish

12
new mammals

2
new birds

Papua New Guinea (PNG)

is one of the least explored countries on the planet. Scientists think there are many species of plants and animals still waiting to be discovered in its cloud forests, incredibly steep, rugged mountains, and thick, steamy jungles, as well as its swamps and floodplains. We know over 700 different tribes of people call it home. PNG covers 178,704 square miles, and includes hundreds of islands. Most of PNG is tropical rain forest – but each year, about 3% of the forest is chopped down.

Let's go exploring

Some places in New Guinea are so remote and hard to reach that you can only get there by plane – it's just too steep, jungly, and slippery for roads. Or you can do as the locals do: paddle down the famous Sepik River in a dugout canoe. The river is 700 miles long, and there is much to see, as many very different tribes live along its shores. Some tribes make amazing wood carvings, and in special rituals many play long wooden garamut drums, hollowed out from tree trunks.

SPEAKING SEPIK

The Sepik River in Papua New Guinea

BEAR SAYS

Traditional tribes teach us how to live with nature without destroying it.

Fabulous tales

The country's national symbol is the raggiana bird-of-paradise. Papua New Guinea has nearly 40 different species of birds-of-paradise. The males are especially fine looking, with the most handsome feathers – some very long, some oddly shaped, others brilliantly colored. The birds ruffle their fabulous feathers and dance crazily, sometimes for hours, to try to attract a lady.

Feeling peckish?

Some tribes in Papua New Guinea used to be cannibals – they would kill their enemies and eat them! Even today, some older people remember eating human flesh.

Slow and steady

Giant tortoises can live much longer than humans. Jonathan is a Seychelles giant tortoise that lives on the island of St. Helena, and is the oldest living land animal. He was born in 1832 – so he's much older than your grandparents.

Cheating death?

Some people have themselves frozen when they die, hoping that one day there will be a cure for whatever killed them. This is called cryonics. It is expensive, so some people just have their brain stored. Dr. James Bedford was the first person to have his body preserved, in 1967. If he is ever revived, maybe he could live to be the oldest man on Earth!

Golden oldies

Macaw parrots can live for more than 80 years.

Some koi fish can live for over 200 years.

Bowhead whales can live up to 200 years.

In New Zealand, tuatara lizards can live more than 100 years.

Can't match this patch
A patch of seagrass in the Mediterranean Sea could be the oldest living thing on Earth. Scientists reckon the seagrass could be more than 100,000 years old. It never dies because it keeps making clones of itself!

OLDEST

Truly old things on and of the Earth

BEAR SAYS
The oldest tree in the world is a 5,066-year-old bristlecone pine.

Clammy contenders
Some clams living in the icy waters off Iceland are more than 400 years old. That means they were sitting around on the bottom of the ocean when William Shakespeare was writing his famous plays. Scientists work out the age of clams by counting the rings on their shells.

The oldest person
The oldest person ever recorded was French woman Jeanne Calment. She died in 1997, aged 122 years, 164 days.

Birth of Earth
The oldest piece of earth on Earth is the Jack Hills in Western Australia (pictured). They are more than 3.6 billion years old. The rocks in the Jack Hills contain bits of a mineral called zircon that are 4.4 billion years old – only slightly younger than the Earth itself.

Dizzy view

If you want a lift into the sky, try the Bailong Elevator in Zhangjiajie, China. It is the world's highest exterior elevator. It is 1,070 feet tall and clings to the side of a cliff. Its glass-fronted cars give a giddy view straight down over a valley.

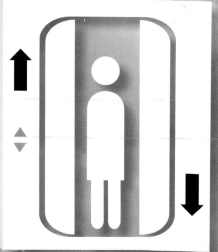

UP IN THE AIR

It's a different world up there!

Flitting to fame

Pretty little tortoiseshell butterflies have been spotted fluttering around the Himalayan mountains, 19,000 feet above sea level – making them the world's highest-flying insects.

Flying around the pole

"Pole flying" is an old ritual that the Totonac people in Mexico still practice. Five men in traditional costumes climb a 90-foot pole. One stays on a platform at the top, playing a flute and drum. The others, tied to the pole by ropes, jump backward off the platform, then "fly" upside down around the pole, down to the ground. Each of the four flying men represents a season, and each flies around the pole 13 times, signifying the 52 weeks of the year.

Clear clouds

You need really good eyes to see the world's highest clouds. They are 47–53 miles above the Earth! They are called "night clouds," or noctilucent clouds, and are made of ice crystals. You can only see these beautiful clouds just after sunset, when the sun shines up on them from below the horizon.

Raising the bar

No other birds fly higher than bar-headed geese, which sometimes wing their way over the world's tallest peak, Mt. Everest, which is 29,029 feet high. It takes them about 8 hours.

Lot of hot air

Every November, near Saga City in Japan, hundreds of brightly colored and oddly shaped balloons take to the sky. The Saga International Balloon Festival is the largest aerial event in Asia, and one of the biggest balloon festivals in the world. The biggest balloon festival is held in Albuquerque, New Mexico, in October — more than 750 balloons float above the ground during the nine-day event.

People no match for speedy goose

While it takes a bar-headed goose about 8 hours to fly over the top of Mt. Everest, it took humans 7 weeks to scale the peak for the first time. New Zealander Edmund Hillary and Tenzing Norgay from Nepal became the first two people to reach the top on May 29, 1953. They had to carry oxygen tanks because it's hard to breathe up there.

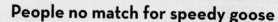

Buzz buzz bumble bird?

The Cuban bee hummingbird is the world's smallest bird. It is so small – only 2 inches long – that people often mistake it for a bee! It weighs a mere 0.06 ounces, and the males are even smaller than the females.

Mellisuga helenae
AVES CUBANAS

Carving a name for himself

Willard Wigan, a sculptor from England, has a good eye. He needs to, as he makes the world's smallest statues. His creations include a Statue of Liberty that fits into the eye of a needle, and a copy of Michelangelo's famous statue of David, carved from a grain of sand. Here is a photo, taken through a microscope, of his statue The Starry Lovers, perched on a diamond ring.

A cupful of lemur

They could easily fit in a teacup, but mouse lemurs are our not-too-distant cousins. These 2.5-inch creatures, from the island of Madagascar, are the smallest primates in the world. They may soon die out because their forest homes are being cut down.

Slowly shrinking

Madagascar is also where you'll find the world's smallest chameleon. The pygmy chameleon is less than 1 inch long and could sit on your fingertip. It started out much bigger thousands of years ago, but shrank over time, probably because food was scarce on the island.

PERFECTLY TINY

The world in miniature

BEAR SAYS

On an expedition, small things can make all the difference: a first-aid kit, compass, and whistle.

Itty bitty city

The world's smallest nation, Vatican City, covers an area about the size of 60 soccer fields — only 110 acres. It has a population the size of a secondary school — about 800 residents, making it also the nation with the smallest population in the world.

Branching out

Imagine having a whole forest living in your house! Bonsai is a Japanese art form that grows miniature versions of real trees. Leaves are pruned, trunks are trimmed, and branches are wired to make the little plants look just like the real thing. Some bonsai trees are only 1–3 inches high.

Thread bare

The world's smallest snake, the Barbados threadsnake, was discovered in 2008 on the island of Barbados. It fits on a coin and is as thin as spaghetti. It only grows about 4 inches long.

Another world

Visiting Socotra Island, in the Indian Ocean, might feel like visiting another planet – and in a way you are. The island has been isolated from the rest of the world for so long that many of its plants have evolved differently from those found anywhere else. Check out these dragon's blood trees!

Knock on stone

The Stone Forest, or Shilin, in China is a huge grouping of tall rock pillars that look like trees. The stone forest covers an area as big as 25,000 baseball diamonds. It was formed 270 million years ago, before dinosaurs were around.

Grandest hole

The Grand Canyon is one of the biggest and most spectacular canyons on Earth. It is certainly the most famous! It was carved by a single river, the Colorado, over millions of years. The main canyon is 227 miles long, 18 miles wide, and up to 1 mile deep.

BEAR SAYS

Armed with the right equipment, you can cook food in Iceland's steaming geysers.

Place of pong

Hverir, in Iceland, is one of the smelliest and strangest-looking places in the world. It is where the center of the Earth is trying to force its way to the surface. Volcanic activity has given it steaming holes in the ground, spouting hot springs called geysers, sulfurous puddles, and stinky mud pools.

WILDEST LANDSCAPES

Some of nature's most extreme and fascinating creations

Sweet, but don't eat

They look good enough to eat, but the Chocolate Hills in the Philippines would taste just like limestone if you bit into one. There are about 1,700 of these almost perfectly shaped little hills. They are covered in grass, which turns chocolate brown during the dry season.

WHAT A WHOPPER!

Giant stars of the animal kingdom

Super sea serpent

Nicknamed the "world's biggest herring," the oarfish is the longest bony fish. It can grow up to 56 feet long. It takes about 15 men to hold a full-grown fish from head to tail. It isn't too scary though – it has no teeth.

Giants walk among us

Giant salamanders live in Japan and China. They are the world's largest amphibians, which are creatures that can live in water or on land. They can grow up to 5 feet 10 inches long – although one in the 17th century was supposedly 33 feet long and ate cows and horses! Warts on their bodies pick up vibrations that help them hunt.

One shell of a clam!

Most clams are small enough to eat by the handful, but giant clams are big enough to swallow a small person whole. Luckily for you, they "clam up" so slowly that you can easily swim away before this happens. That's probably why there are no records of anyone being gobbled by a clam. Not yet, anyway.

BEAR SAYS

I have a healthy respect for large wild animals. Always be sure to treat them with caution and respect – they can be very dangerous!

Mom, I'm thirsty again

Human babies drink about 25 fluid ounces a day. That's just a dribble compared to the world's biggest baby, the blue whale. Blue whale calves gulp down 1,400 cups of milk a day and stack on about 200 pounds every 24 hours – as much as a large man weighs! At birth, a blue whale calf is almost as long as a bus.

Growing into its legs

The giant African millipede is the world's longest millipede. It is born with only about 14 legs. As it grows, it adds more legs. By the time it reaches its adult length – up to 15 inches – it can have as many as 100 legs.

WANTED
ALIVE

Name: Tiger
Lives: Asia
Prefers: Mountains and forests
Number in wild: About 3,500
Threatened by: Hunting; habitat loss
Comments: 3 tiger subspecies became extinct in the past 60 years

WANTED
ALIVE

Name: Kakapo
Lives: New Zealand
Prefers: Forests and woodland
Number in the wild: About 125
Threatened by: Habitat loss; dogs, cats, and rats
Comments: World's heaviest parrot; can't fly; nocturnal. Breeding programs underway

WANTED
ALIVE

Name: Javan rhino
Lives: Java
Prefers: Thick forests
Number in wild: About 50
Threatened by: Hunting; habitat loss
Comments: Its relative the Sumatran rhino is also highly endangered

WANTED
ALIVE

Name: Bluefin tuna
Lives: Atlantic, Pacific, Indian, and Southern Oceans
Number in wild: 25,000 in Atlantic Ocean, and tens of thousands in the Pacific Ocean – but fishing takes many thousands every year
Threatened by: Overfishing
Comments: A single tuna can sell for $100,000. That's why 11,000 tons are caught every year

ANIMALS IN DANGER

Some creatures are in a whole world of trouble

WANTED

ALIVE

Name: Orange-bellied parrot
Lives: Tasmania and Victoria, Australia
Prefers: Coastal grasslands
Number in wild: About 20
Threatened by: Habitat loss; species competition
Comments: Breeding programs underway

Also threatened with extinction:
Addax, Niger
Amur leopard, Russia
Blue-throated macaw, Bolivia
Iberian lynx, Spain
Saola, Vietnam and Laos

WANTED

ALIVE

Name: Leatherback turtle
Lives: Pacific and Atlantic Oceans
Number in wild: About 2,300 adult females in Pacific Ocean; Atlantic Ocean numbers are dropping
Threatened by: Marine pollution, especially plastic bags; fishing
Comments: This largest sea turtle has survived 100 million years

BEAR SAYS

Every single day, as many as 5 plant or animal species become extinct.

Super bug

If you want to live in a really, really cold place, you'd be best off being a bacteria. *Deinococcus radiodurans* is a bacteria that is almost indestructible. It survives extreme cold, extreme heat, and extreme radiation!

Earning cold herd cash

The Nenet people of Siberia probably work in the coldest conditions in the world. They move huge herds of reindeer thousands of miles through the Arctic Circle. Temperatures often drop to −58°F as the Nenets and their animals cross freezing plains and rivers.

COLDEST

Chill out in the coolest spots on Earth!

BEAR SAYS

When you're in the wild and it's icy cold, make sure you stay dry. Carry spare warm clothes.

Frosty reception for guests

Every winter in Jukkasjärvi, Sweden, thousands of people pay to sleep on blocks of ice. That's because they are staying at the world's first and largest ice hotel. The hotel is built every winter out of blocks of ice from the nearby Torne River – and then the building disappears when summer comes and the ice melts. Guests keep snug by sleeping on reindeer skins.

Living in a freezer

Russia is the biggest country in the world, and also the world's coldest country. Its average temperature is 22.1°F, as most of the country is much closer to the North Pole than to the Equator. In some parts it is so cold, you could throw boiling water into the cold air and it would explode into vapor and ice.

Fantasy land

You might not want to vacation in a city where the temperature drops to −22°F, the wind howls in from Siberia, and it gets dark just after lunch, but a million people do every year. They aren't in Harbin, China, for the weather, but to enjoy the ice and snow festival (pictured) – one of the biggest and coolest ice festivals in the world. There are hundreds of buildings and sculptures made from ice – some of them bigger than soccer fields. At night, colorful lights and lasers turn the festival into an amazing wonderland.

−459.67°F
Absolutely freezing

Did you know there is a minimum temperature where it can't get any colder? That temperature is −459.67°F, or 0° kelvin (absolute zero). In 2003, scientists created the coldest temperature ever – only 0.0000000005°C above absolute zero.

We're all Rip Van Winkle
On average, if you live to the age of 60, you will have spent more than 20 years asleep!

5 most populated countries
1 China 1,382,402,000
2 India 1,327,001,000
3 United States 324,148,000
4 Indonesia 260,619,000
5 Brazil 209,590,000

5 least populated countries
1 Vatican City 800
2 Nauru 10,000
3 Tuvalu 10,000
4 Palau 21,000
5 San Marino 32,000

Long live the people
If you are born in the small European country of Andorra, you can expect to live for 82.4 years – longer than anywhere else on Earth. The next longest-living people are the Japanese, who live on average for 82.2 years.

Reach for the sky
The Dutch are the world's tallest people. Dutch men on average are 6 feet 1 inch, while Dutch women are 5 feet 7 inches.

16–20 ft.
Giraffe
Average height

World's shortest people
The Mbuti, from Congo, are the shortest people on Earth. Their average height is 4 feet 6 inches.

6 ft. 1 in.
Dutch people
Average male height

4 ft. 6 in.
Mbuti people
Average male height

BEAR SAYS

You don't have to be big and tall to be tough. You just need to keep on trying.

PEOPLE POWER

Surprising statistics about us humans

7 billion
That's how many people live on planet Earth.

214,000
That's how much the Earth's human population is increasing every day.

Sitting pretty

The Wodaabé people in Niger, Africa, do things a little differently. Instead of young women entering beauty pageants, it's the young men who put on makeup and their finest threads, during the Cure Salée (Salt Cure) festival, to try and find a wife.

NEED FOR SPEED

Things that go really FAST!

Lot of bull

The world's "fastest festival" could be San Fermin, held every July in Pamplona, Spain. It is certainly one of the deadliest! A whole lot of men, dressed in white, are chased through narrow streets by angry bulls wearing clanking cowbells. Since 1910, at least 16 people have been killed during "the running of the bulls," and 200 badly injured.

How fast is a cheetah?

Cheetah: 109 yards in 5.95 seconds

Athlete: 109 yards in 9.58 seconds

Cheetah: 0–60 mph in 3 seconds

Ferrari: 0–60 mph in 3.5 seconds

BEAR SAYS

In Siberia, I made a toboggan out of yak hide, but a tea tray would do the job, too!

Going downhill

The fastest sport on Earth, without using an engine, is downhill speed skiing. Brave (or crazy) skiers tuck themselves up tight and race down steep snowy hills at up to 156 mph. In 1997, American Jeff Hamilton fell at 151 mph. Amazingly, he shattered only three small bones – but he did get terrible snow burn.

The fastest living things

5.57 mph
Fastest running insect
Australian tiger beetle

SIX-LEGGED SPEEDSTER: The fastest-running insect, the Australian tiger beetle, travels at 5.57 mph. That may not sound fast, but that's about 170 body lengths per second. Or you running at 340 mph!

27.44 mph
Fastest person
Usain Bolt

MOTOR MAN: The Jamaican sprinter Usain Bolt is the quickest man ever timed. He holds the world record for the fastest 100-meter sprint, with a top speed of 27.44 mph. But even Bolt could not keep up that pace for more than a few seconds.

35 mph
Fastest flying insect
Dragonfly

WONDER WINGS: Large dragonflies can fly at up to 35 mph for short bursts. They have slender bodies, two pairs of strong, transparent wings, and can move in any direction, including backward.

68 mph
Fastest fish
Sailfish

FLEET FISH: Sailfish are the oceans' kings and queens of speed. These 10-foot fish can swim at 68 mph. They use the huge sail that runs along their back to make themselves look even bigger, scaring little fish together into larger herds to gobble up.

70 mph
Fastest mammal
Cheetah

A BLUR OF FUR: Imagine you are the fastest sprinter in the world. If you were trying to escape a cheetah and the nearest tree to climb was 328 feet away, the cheetah would beat you there, even if it was twice as far away when you both started running.

106 mph
Fastest bird (level flight)
Spine-tailed swift

SWIFT BY NATURE: These speedy birds spend most of their lives in the air, feeding on the insects they can catch in their wide beaks. This attention-seeking swift sets the bird record for level flight during mating displays.

200 mph
Fastest bird (diving)
Peregrine falcon

FLASH FALCON: Lucky you are not a bird, or you might be in the sights of a peregrine falcon. These hunters like to catch other birds while they're flying, swooping down on them at 200 mph. They are the fastest birds and the fastest animals in the world.

That's crazy!

Skydivers usually jump from planes with their parachutes strapped to their backs. But in banzai skydiving you throw your parachute out of the plane, then leap out after it, freediving for a while before trying to catch it!

BORN TO BE WILD

Thrills and spills from around the world

Fastest flying squirrel

Wingsuits are like special jumpsuits. Put one on and you can fly like a bird, or perhaps a squirrel, as they are also nicknamed "flying squirrel suits." Jumping from a height of 32,000 feet, a Japanese wingsuit pilot called Shin Ito set a few new world records in 2011: the longest wingsuit flight (14.4 miles), the longest flight time (5 minutes 22 seconds), and the fastest speed – an incredible 226 mph!

Having a vine time

The "land divers" of Pentecost Island in Vanuatu were the world's first bungee jumpers. Every year, between April and June, young men jump from tall wooden platforms, with vines tied to their ankles to stop them hitting the ground. They sky-dive to show their bravery and to celebrate the yam crop. Let's hope those vines are strong!

Ride 'em cowboy

The Calgary Stampede in Canada is the world's largest rodeo, a 10-day-long festival held in July. There are pancake breakfasts, barbecues, and even chuckwagon racing. More than a million people visit "The Greatest Outdoor Show on Earth" every year.

Rolling on

Invented in New Zealand in 1994, a zorb is like a hamster ball for kids. You jump inside a big plastic ball and roll yourself down a grassy hill. Water zorbing is the same thing but (you guessed it) on water.

SECRETS FROM BELOW

Hidden treasures from beneath the earth and sea

BEAR SAYS

When you're at sea, wear a life jacket, watch the weather, and always have a plan.

Titanic discovery

In 1985, the wreck of the Titanic was discovered at the bottom of the Atlantic Ocean. The giant ocean liner hit an iceberg and sunk on its very first voyage from London to New York in 1912, even though it was supposed to be "unsinkable." Some of the items recovered from the wreck include perfume bottles, bottles of beer and wine, a deck chair, letters from passengers, menus from the last meal served, jewelry, and clothes.

Elusive glittering prize

No wonder gold costs so much. Only 177,000 tons of gold have ever been mined. It would all fit in a room 55 feet square. Gold can be hammered into sheets so thin that a stack of 7,000 of them would be only as thick as a coin. And 1 ounce of gold could be stretched out as a wire 50 miles long!

55 ft.

Sea how they stand

Children stand silently in a ring, holding hands. But you'll need to put on a bathing suit and wear goggles to see them. They are part of an underwater sculpture garden at Moliniere Bay, in Grenada, that sits on the ocean floor 22 feet below the surface. The 65 figures are casts of residents who live in the nearby towns.

Get-rich scheme

If you want to get rich, work out a way of getting gold out of seawater. There are 20 million tons of gold in the world's oceans. It's just that no one knows how to get to it yet!

Diamonds really are forever

If you go diamond hunting, look for a place where there have been lots of volcanoes. Most diamonds are formed deep below the Earth's surface under huge pressure and high temperature. They are brought to the surface by volcanic eruptions. Many diamonds are almost as old as the planet. Some can be more than 3 billion years old.

All packed in

Almost 77,700 people live in each square mile of Mumbai in India, making it the most densely populated city on the planet. Per square mile, there are 26,400 people in New York City, 13,200 people in London, 9,700 people in Berlin, and 5,400 people in Sydney.

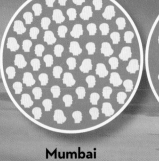

Mumbai
77,700 people

New York
26,400 people

London
13,200 people

Berlin
9,700 people

Sydney
5,400 people

151 gallons
How much water each person in the US uses each day.

3 gallons
How much water each person in Ethiopia uses each day.

TOP 10 DIRTY CITIES

Cities can be dirty, polluted places with air that can harm you. The 10 cities with the worst air pollution, according to the World Health Organization, are:

1 Ahvaz, Iran

2 Ulaanbaatar, Mongolia

3 Sanandaj, Iran

4 Ludhiana, India

5 Quetta, Pakistan

6 Kermanshah, Iran

7 Peshawar, Pakistan

8 Gaborone, Botswana

9 Yasouj, Iran

10 Kanpur, India

LIFE IN THE CITY

Fascinating facts about where most of us live

BEAR SAYS

Survival skills are the same in the city as the wild: keep your eyes and ears open and stay alert!

Middle East Manhattan

You might think skyscrapers are very modern, but in the Middle East people have been building them for hundreds of years! In Yemen, people in the town of Shibam live in mud buildings that soar towards the heavens. Some buildings are 11 stories tall. They were built this way to protect locals from attacks by desert people called Bedouins. The town is sometimes called the "Manhattan of the desert."

Twisty tale

Every Easter Sunday, people race tricycles down Lombard Street in San Francisco. Most of them fall off before the bottom, because it is the crookedest street on Earth. Its sharp corners have featured in lots of movies and television shows.

Site for sore legs

Baldwin Street, in the New Zealand city of Dunedin, is the world's steepest residential street, which at its steepest rises 3.3 feet for every 9.9 feet you travel on it. Every year, 1,000 runners rush to the top and back again in the Baldwin Street Gutbuster race. An easier competition is the Jaffa Race, in which 30,000 candies are rolled down the hill for charity.

Duck out for a game

Pato, the national game of Argentina, is a mix of polo and basketball. The players ride horses — and in the old days they used a duck instead of a ball! Riders were often trampled under the horses' hooves or killed in knife fights when the games got too exciting.

ANIMAL CAPERS

Creatures big and small are extremely sporty

Jumbo pileup on polo field

Giant piles of poop on the field are a big problem when playing elephant polo. The ball often gets stuck in them and someone has to dig it out! Elephant polo was first played in India 100 years ago, when the British started using the huge brainy beasts instead of horses. There are three jumbos on each team. Each elephant has two passengers — one to steer it and one to hit the ball into the goal. There are three international tournaments, in Nepal, Sri Lanka, and Thailand.

Mush, mush!

The longest dogsled race in the world is held every March in Alaska. Dogs taking part in the Iditarod have to run 1,049 miles, pulling a sled through blizzards and freezing temperatures. The race usually takes between 9 and 15 days.

Bumping off opponents

There's lots of bumping going on during the annual camel wrestling championship in Selçuk, Turkey. Two male camels fight it out for the right to spend a little time with a nearby female camel. Although the wrestling match is often quite tame, the camels sometimes take off into the crowd, scattering spectators.

Riding Big Bird

Ostriches are the biggest birds in the world – but did you know some people like to hop onto their backs and race them? Ostrich racing is very common in Africa, especially in Oudtshoorn, in South Africa, where professional jockeys jump on board, then hang on to the bird's feathers and neck for dear life as they race around an oval track.

Slow and steady

The slowest sport in the world is snail racing. The slimy garden creatures start in the middle of a 13-inch-wide circle and "race" toward the edge. The record time to complete the race is 2 minutes 20 seconds!

Greatest wall EVER

The Great Wall of China is the longest thing people have ever built. It goes for about 5,500 miles – although not all of it is connected. Some parts were built more than 2,000 years ago, but the most famous bits were built between 1368 and 1644. Bits of it have been rebuilt many times. When the wall was being built, it was nicknamed "the longest cemetery on Earth," because so many people died constructing it.

Great Wall of China

Rosy city really rocks

You may have seen the ancient city of Petra in the film *Indiana Jones and the Last Crusade*. Petra is on the edge of the Arabian Desert, in Jordan. Much of it, including 800 elaborate graves, was carved into rose-colored rock cliffs about 2,000 years ago.

Petra

He's one big dude

An awesome statue called Christ the Redeemer stands on top of a mountain and watches over the people of Rio de Janeiro in Brazil. The statue is as tall as a 10-story building and its arms are as wide as two buses. There are small spikes on the statue's head to stop birds landing and making a mess.

Christ the Redeemer

Mayan marvel

The city of Chichén Itzá, in Mexico, was a center of Mayan civilization up to CE 1200. You can still see its pyramids and temples; star observatory; carvings of sacred feathered serpents, jaguars, and warriors; a well that people were thrown into to please the gods; and ball courts where brutal games were played. The Temple of Kukulkan has 365 stone steps, one for each day of the year. During the spring and autumn equinox, when the sun hits the stone steps, it makes a shadow shaped like a snake.

Chichén Itzá

Monument to love

Imagine loving your wife so much you built one of the world's most beautiful buildings for her. That's what Indian emperor Shah Jahan did when his wife died in 1631. His memorial to his wife, the Taj Mahal, took 22 years and 22,000 people to build. According to legend, Shah Jahan then had the hands of the architect and craftsmen chopped off so they could never create another building like it.

Taj Mahal

BEAR SAYS

Without teamwork we would never have built anything. Together, we can build wonders!

7 MAN-MADE WONDERS

These Wonders of the World are truly amazing

Colossal day out

A day at the Colosseum in Rome was quite a spectacle almost 2,000 years ago. Rome's residents would turn up at the stadium in the morning. First, they could watch wild animals, such as lions and bears, being hunted. Over lunch they could watch prisoners being executed, then in the afternoon they could enjoy blood-thirsty gladiator fights.

Colosseum

Cloud-shrouded mystery

Up in the mountains of Peru sit the ruins of Machu Picchu. It is known as the "Lost City of the Incas," because nobody except local people knew about it until 1911. The city was built from stone around CE 1450, but was abandoned only 100 years later — no one knows why. The buildings were so well constructed that you can't slip a knife between the joins in the stones. The city was built from huge rocks hauled up the steep mountains over great distances.

Machu Picchu

A taste of space

How would you like to float above the Earth, just like an astronaut? That's what happens during "zero gravity" flights, when a plane flies in a big semicircle to counteract gravity. The US and Russia use zero gravity flights to train their astronauts, but now anyone can find out what it's like to travel in a "vomit comet" – if they have enough money – and a strong stomach!

Lodger from outer space

The Hoba is a giant 67-ton iron meteorite that landed in Namibia, Africa, about 80,000 years ago. It is the largest meteorite ever found.

Eyes on the skies

The world's largest optical telescope scans the skies from the Canary Islands, in the Atlantic Ocean. The telescope has a mirror 34 feet wide. A new European telescope that is still being built will have a lens as wide as five buses placed end to end, and will contain more glass than all the other telescopes in the world combined. It will be so powerful that astronomers will be able to see the lunar rover that was left on the Moon in 1971.

BEAR SAYS

The first man in space was the Russian cosmonaut Yuri Gagarin, in 1961.

Dark side of the Moon

When *Apollo 13* rounded the far side of the Moon on April 15, 1970, its three astronauts, James Lovell, John Swigert, and Fred Haise, were 249,205 miles from Earth – the farthest away anyone has ever been.

Pocket rocket money

If you are going into outer space on a rocket, don't forget to take a dollar or two. Scientists have designed money, called the Quasi Universal Intergalactic Denomination, or Quid, to be used by space travelers.

OUT OF THIS WORLD

Star attractions from the galaxy and beyond

Seeing little green men

Each year in July, aliens descend on the town of Roswell, New Mexico. The scary extraterrestrials are really only people dressed up as space creatures to attend the Roswell UFO Festival. Roswell was where some people say a flying saucer crashed one night in 1947.

Vanishing point

Gedi, in Kenya, is a mysterious lost city that was suddenly abandoned in the 1600s. Gedi was very advanced, with running water and flushing toilets. Archeologists found Chinese Ming vases, Venetian glass, and other items from all around the world in the city. No one knows why its inhabitants vanished or where they went.

Lost Atlantis

Explorers have searched for the fabled lost city of Atlantis. They've looked everywhere... Santorini, Greece: FAIL. Off the coast of Morocco; off the coast of Cuba; under the South Pole: FAIL. Keep looking, guys!

Marvel of Micronesia

Nan Madol is a ruined city that lies off the island of Pohnpei in Micronesia. It is often called the "Venice of the Pacific" because its 90 human-made islands are linked by canals.

LOST WORLDS

Great civilizations and cities that time forgot

What a wonder

The world's most amazing Hindu architecture is found at Angkor Wat, a huge ancient temple in Cambodia that covers 494 acres – about the same area as 300 soccer fields. The temple was abandoned for hundreds of years and swallowed up by the jungle.

Great big heads

As early as 1500 BCE, the Olmec people of Mexico began building big city-temple complexes, such as the one at Tenochtitlán. The Olmecs are famous for their massive stone heads, nicknamed "Colossal Heads" – some are nearly 10 feet tall and weigh more than 22 tons.

Living in luxury

Luxor, in Egypt, is nicknamed the "world's greatest open air museum." It contains Thebes, which was Egypt's capital 3,500 years ago – and some of the most amazing ancient temples in the world. King Tutankhamun's tomb, filled with gold and riches, was discovered in 1922 in the nearby Valley of the Kings.

Colossus of Crete

Knossos is a huge palace on the island of Crete, which was the cradle of ancient Minoan civilization about 4,000 years ago. In the basement of the palace was a labyrinth, where a minotaur – an animal that was half human and half bull – was supposedly imprisoned. The magnificence of the Minoans was only discovered when the palace was dug up in 1900.

✕
BEAR
SAYS

Learning about the past is one of the greatest adventures we can set out on.

DEADEST

Turning them in their graves

Every seven years, the Malagasy people in Madagascar dig up dead relatives and hold a big celebration. During the "Turning of the Bones" ceremony (*Famadihana*) they wrap the dead people up in fresh silk cloth and dance with their bodies around the tomb. Then they return the bodies to their graves.

Seeing stars

The deadest place to get buried might well be outer space. At least it is dead quiet there! These days you can have your ashes placed in a tube the size of a lipstick case and have them blasted into space on a rocket ship. One famous person buried in space was Gene Roddenberry, creator of *Star Trek*.

This city is pretty dead

You have to be dead keen to visit the "City of the Dead," near the remote village of Dargavs in Russia. These strange little houses are over 400 years old. So are some of their "residents," who holed themselves up inside and died of a dreadful disease called the plague. You can still see skulls, bones, and half-mummified bodies in the houses, which are actually stone family burial crypts. Local legend still says that anyone who visits here dies.

Big date with death

The deadest day on the Mexican calendar is the Day of the Dead on November 2nd. Funnily enough, the locals consider it a happy day. They visit the graves of dead relatives and bring them gifts, such as flowers, their favorite food and drinks, and toy or candy skulls and skeletons. Some even have a picnic at the graves and a sing-along.

BEAR SAYS

On the Day of the Dead, people give each other skulls made out of chocolate or sugar.

A frightfully ghoulish month

For Chinese people, the deadest month is their seventh lunar month. They call it Ghost Month. During this time, the gates of Hell are flung open, allowing the souls of the dead to roam the Earth and pester the living for 30 days and nights. Many temples hold ceremonies where they light lanterns, burn incense, offer food to the ghosts, and say prayers. During the Hungry Ghost Festival, people also put on opera and puppet shows to entertain the ghosts.

Sleeping with the fishes

The Neptune Memorial Reef, which opened in 2007 off of Florida, is the world's biggest underwater mausoleum. The cemetery is a recreation of the mythical lost city of Atlantis. There are plaques, columns, pathways, statues of lions, and even benches to sit on in your wet suit. People's ashes are mixed into the concrete structures of the underwater city.

INDEX

Bear Grylls
EXTREME PLANET
Exploring the Most Extreme Stuff on Earth

First American Edition 2017
Kane Miller, A Division of EDC Publishing

Conceived by Weldon Owen in partnership with Bear Grylls Ventures

Produced by Weldon Owen, Suite 3.08 The Plaza, 535 King's Road, London SW10 0SZ, UK

Copyright © 2016 Weldon Owen, an imprint of Kings Road Publishing

For information contact:
Kane Miller, A Division of EDC Publishing
PO Box 470663
Tulsa, OK 74147-0663
www.kanemiller.com
www.edcpub.com
www.usbornebooksandmore.com

Library of Congress Control Number: 2017945576

Printed in Malaysia
1 2 3 4 5 6 7 8 9 10

ISBN: 978-1-61067-754-7

KIDS – if you want to try any of the activities in this book, please ask your parents first! Parents – all outdoor activities carry some degree of risk and we recommend that anyone participating in these activities be aware of the risks involved and seek professional instruction and guidance. None of the health/medical information in this book is intended as a substitute for professional medical advice; always seek the advice of a qualified practitioner.

DISCLAIMER
Weldon Owen and Bear Grylls take pride in doing their best to get the facts right in putting together the information in this book, but occasionally something slips past their beady eyes. Therefore we make no warranties about the accuracy or completeness of the information in the book and to the maximum extent permitted, we disclaim all liability. Wherever possible, we will endeavor to correct any errors of fact at reprint.

PICTURE CREDITS
While every effort has been made to credit all contributors, Owen would like to apologize should there have been any o[...] errors, and would be pleased to make any appropriate corre[...] future editions of this book.

All images below from Shutterstock.com
©ActiveLines; ©2630ben; ©3drenderings; ©Albo; ©Aleksandrs Bondars; ©Aleksey Vanin; ©Alex Staroseltsev; ©Alexander Raths; ©Alexyz3d; ©Ana Vasileva; ©Andrei Nekrassov; ©Andrey_Kuzmin; ©Anna Kulikova; ©Anton Balazh; ©Art House; ©Ase; ©Ati design; ©Benoit Daoust; ©Betabaqe; ©Brandon Bourdages; ©Byelikova Oksana; ©Cameramannz; ©Catmando; ©cellistka; ©Chekky; ©Christian Weber; ©Colin Edwards Wildside; ©corbac40; ©Cortyn; ©Cosmin Manci; ©Crystal Eye Studio; ©CS Stock; ©Dario Lo Presti; ©defpicture; ©Dejan Stanisavljevic; ©derter; ©Digital Storm; ©DigitalHand Studio; ©Dirk Ercken; ©Dr. Morley Read; ©DVARG; ©Eduard Radu; ©Elenamiv; ©Elenarts; ©Elesey; ©Eric Isselee; ©Evlakhov Valeriy; ©eye-blink; ©fivespots; ©goldnetz; ©Guan jiangchi; ©Hellen Grig; ©Iconic Bestiary; ©iFerol; ©Igor Kovalchuk; ©IhorZigor; ©Imaake; ©imnoom; ©Incredible Arctic; ©James BO Insogna; ©Jan Cejka; ©Jan Martin Will; ©Jaromir Chalabala; ©Jin Yong; ©Jorg Hackemann; Jos Beltman; Joseph Sohm; ©Jurik; ©Peter; ©Kevin Key; ©KittyVector; ©Kletr; ©Krisztian; ©Lena Lir; ©Lena Serditova; ©leungchopan; ©luckypic; ©Magnia; ©mapichai; ©Mario Hagen; ©Martin Maun; ©Miceking; ©Migel; ©mistral9; ©Murat Cokeker; ©Nagib; ©NatalieJean; ©NEILRAS; ©nikolae; ©notkoo; ©Olga Reznik; ©Osokin Aleksandr; ©ostill; ©Pakhnyushchy; ©Pan Xunbin; ©pandapaw; ©Pavel Burchenko; ©PavloArt Studio; ©Phant; ©Piotr Snigorski; ©R Gombarik; ©R. Formidable; ©RCPPHOTO; ©RedKoala; ©Reinke Fox; ©Rich Carey; ©Ridkous Mykhailo; ©S-F; ©Sanit Fuangnakhon; ©Scott Rothstein; ©Sergey Kohl; ©Sergey Uryadnikov; ©skelos; ©Skunkeye; ©Somprasong Khrueaphan; ©srbh karthik; ©Stanislav Fosenbauer; ©Stefano Garau; ©Super Prin; ©Sviluppo; ©tanatat; ©tashechka; ©Tawee wongdee; ©Theeradech Sanin; ©tovovan; ©Triduza Studio; ©Ursa Major; ©Valentyna Chukhlyebova; ©Vector Goddess; ©Vertyr; ©violetkaipa; ©Vladimir Melnik; ©Weenee; ©weltreisendertj; ©yunus85; ©Zaichenko Olga

ILLUSTRATIONS
All illustrations by James Gulliver Hancock/The Jacky Winter Group.
All illustrations copyright Weldon Owen Publishing

Discover more amazing books in the Bear Grylls series:

Bear Grylls Survival Camp
Survival Skills Handbook (Volume I)

Polar Worlds Activity Book
Wild Survival Activity Book
Animal Detective Activity Book
Dangerous Animals Activity Book
In the Jungle Coloring Book
Reptiles and Amphibians Coloring Book

Bear Grylls Adventures: The Desert Challenge
Bear Grylls Adventures: The Blizzard Challenge
Bear Grylls Adventures: The Jungle Challenge
Bear Grylls Adventures: The Sea Challenge